Laura Cooke Barker

Society Silhouettes

A Collection of Short Stories

Laura Cooke Barker

Society Silhouettes
A Collection of Short Stories

ISBN/EAN: 9783744705080

Printed in Europe, USA, Canada, Australia, Japan

Cover: Foto ©Thomas Meinert / pixelio.de

More available books at **www.hansebooks.com**

SOCIETY
SILHOUETTES

Collection of Short Stories

BY

LAURA COOKE BARKER

THE HELMAN-TAYLOR COMPANY

CLEVELAND

1898

CONTENTS.

___

A Search for Sensations,   -   -   7

The Senator's Wooing,   -   -   118

Keeping Up Appearances,   -   - 145

The Touch of Nature,   -   -   172

Barbara's Emancipation,   -   - 203

A Twentieth Century Romance,   228

A Search for Sensations.

THE March wind shrieked about the corners of the house and rattled the windows like some restless spirit clamoring for admittance. Occasionally a puff of smoke showed that it found an entrance down the chimney and caused Miss Darlington to push her chair further back from the fireplace.

Only the flickering flames illumined the room and dimly outlined the woman's sweet face as she sat anxiously watching her younger sister, who paced restlessly about the small room, her head thrown back defiantly.

" Don't do it, Dorris, it will bring you anything but happiness!"

Her sister laughed as she stooped to pick up the bit of crumpled paper on the floor. "Happiness!" she exclaimed. "What *is* 'happiness'? *I* have never seen it! Father and mother spent their youth in a battle for daily bread, even when Aunt died and left them her few thousand dollars, it did not bring happiness. No, I wont speak of that. Father's name is still a sacred memory to me, but it killed mother and caused his death, too, I believe, and now we are left to a mere existence on the little that still remains and which permits us to live in this shabby genteel way! What is before us? Nothing, unless it is a chance to marry some good, respectable young clerk on small pay and repeat the history of our father and mother! Ugh! I will *not* do that! This is a chance that will never come to me again and I'm going to take it. I'm tired of a poverty-stricken exist-tence!"

"Mere existence may be tame, but it is not misery, Dorris, and any woman who outrages her nature by marrying as you propose to do is preparing for herself untold wretchedness!"

"Nonsense! Where is the 'untold

wretchedness' in marrying a dear old goose like John Dryden? Love him? Of course I don't, but that's nothing; I never have—and never will—love any one but you—and myself!"

She glanced again at the paper in her hands. " What can I want that he will not give me? Riches untold—the independence which marriage gives to a woman—endless new sensations, in fact!"

Louise sighed, taking the girl's hand in hers. " Dorris, dear," she said, wistfully, "for twenty years I have loved and watched over you! I remember when you were a tiny tot, with golden curls and willful ways. For the sake of those long years of devotion, I ask you not to do this awful thing. It is selling yourself —your womanhood——" she broke off abruptly.

" What a prude you are, Sissy! You were born to be a decorous old maid, but *I* was born to *live*, to enjoy, to stir the world, and I'm going to do it by the

use of John Dryden's millions! Call it
sin if you will; sin is always pleasant. I
have often thought Mephistopheles must
be a charming fellow. Perhaps I shall
make his acquaintance after I have ' sold
myself '—who knows!"

She opened the door as she spoke.

" I'm going to write ' Yes!' In my
hands he will be the golden key to unlock
for me the wonders of a world."

The door closed behind her and Miss
Darlington heard her singing carelessly,
as she mounted the stairs to her own
room.

''Has the child a heart?'' she whispered
to herself. " Mother used to say she had
not, but I fancied it was only her light-
heartedness that made her seem so frivolous and flippant; yet now——?''

She paused in her walk to listen. The
footsteps overhead had ceased—Dorris
was writing the fateful letter.

Miss Darlington shivered, moving
closer to the fire with an involuntary

movement, while her eyes filled with sudden tears.

" Oh, Dorris, Dorris! I would that you were still my baby sister, the golden-haired, innocent sunbeam of my life!" And outside, the March winds moaned as if in sympathy with her pain.

CHAPTER II.

Miss Darlington sat alone at the break-fast table. The morning sunlight streamed in at the bay window, giving the room a cheery brightness, and flooding with its warmth a small dog that lay curled upon the window cushions.

Miss Darlington sipped her coffee and nibbled her muffin, while she gazed at the picture of content which he presented.

" I wish I could forget my troubles as easily as Laddie does," she sighed, rising at last and ringing the bell for her maid.

" Now, Miss Darlington, shure an' ye ain't a thinkin' o' doin with that bit an' sup till lunch?" cried a hearty voice from the doorway.

" Yes, it's all I could eat, Kitty, but you may take up a nice breakfast to Miss Dorris, and tell her it's nearly ten o'clock."

Kitty's brow darkened. She had lived with them for many years and considered herself one of the family, almost.

"It's always Miss Dorris an' niver yoursilf that gets the aisy things o' life!" she muttered, but a quiet glance silenced her, as she removed the untasted breakfast.

" Kitty's impertinence is getting very troublesome," murmured the girl, seating herself beside the dog and pulling his long ears. " Seems to me everything gets to be troublesome, Laddie."

Laddie opened one eye, feebly wagged his tail, and, considering this was all that good manners required by way of reply, continued his doze.

Suddenly Miss Darlington's attention was drawn to a carriage, which finally came to a standstill before her own house. Her heart beat rapidly as she watched the footman descend and open the door. Yes, it was John Dryden! He must have received her sister's note in the morning's mail, and here he was, as eager a lover as if his hair were not grey, nor crow's feet grew about his eyes—and Dorris was still in bed!

Running breathlessly upstairs,she burst into her sister's room.

" Quick, Dorris, Mr. Dryden has come to see you ; do hurry and get up, child ; he is waiting !"

Dorris was sitting up among the pillows, leisurely enjoying her breakfast. " Let him wait," she said, calmly. " It's good for him to begin in the right way. He'll have lots of waiting to do later on."

" Aren't you coming down at all?"

" Oh, yes," she answered, yawning, " but there's no such mad haste. He was a goose to come rushing here at this time in the morning !"

Miss Darlington turned to go down stairs again, her very back expressive of such strong disapprobation that Dorris laughed. " I'll trust him to your tender mercies, my love !" she called after the retreating form, but her sister would not reply.

Kitty had admitted the elderly lover,

and Miss Darlington found him pacing
up and down the little drawing-room.
He turned eagerly as she entered, but
the disappointment in his face showed
he had expected to see Dorris.

" My sister will be down soon," began
Miss Darlington, rather stiffly, and then,
as she read the honest love in the face
before her, she held out her hands with
simple earnestness. " I feel that you
have done her a great honor in asking
her to be your wife, Mr. Dryden, but I
fear she is too young to know her own
mind. She can not understand, as yet,
the real meaning of love. She is only a
frivolous girl. I am so afraid she will not
bring you the happiness you hope for! "

John Dryden pressed the hands he
held.

" Have no fear of that," he answered
quickly. "I know she is only a child, a
frivolous girl, as you put it, but I—er—I
think that is why I am so fond of her,
you know!"

Miss Darlington looked at him as he

stood before her. An old man, tall, thin, with narrow, stooped shoulders, yet with the fire of youth in his eyes. Truly, it was a picture to make the gods laugh, or weep, to see the dignity of age so bound and fettered in the flowery chains of frivolous Cupid.

She motioned to a chair and seated herself at her work table. She knew the dawdling ways of her younger sister, and felt she was in for a prolonged tete-e-tete with her future brother-in-law.

It grew almost impossible to sustain the conversation, however, as the slightest sound drew her companion's attention to the door, with evident disregard of what she was saying, and at last they heard light footsteps on the stairs.

" Dorris is coming," she said, rising and holding out her hand to him once more, "but before I go I want to warn you against the step you are taking. She is a mere child, and you, forgive me, are no longer young. She does not love you

as she should. I doubt if she ever will.
Do you realize all this?"

The hand that held hers trembled. " I
realize it all," he murmured. " Thank
you for your honesty. I know you mean
to be generous, but—but—I *love* her, Miss
Darlington. I would rather be miserable
with her than wretched *without* her."

Miss Darlington was silenced. " You
do love her," she said softly.

" Heavens ! what long faces! Are
you talking about me, I'd like to know?"
the gay young voice broke in upon them,
and Miss Darlington watched John
Dryden's face as he turned to greet her
sister.

" He is happy now, at any rate," she
thought to herself, as she left them alone
together.

An hour later, Dorris danced into the
sitting-room, where she sat sewing.

" Look ! Look ! Look !" she cried,
flashing an immense solitaire before the
other's eyes. " Isn't that worth a few
kisses and silly little speeches?"

" Dorris, if you talk like that, I shall —I shall despise you !"

Dorris laughed. "You don't show much interest in my changed fortunes, my dear; you haven't asked when the great event is to come off. Aren't you at least curious?"

" Do you mean that you have already set the time for your marriage?"

Dorris nodded.

" It's to be in six weeks. I'm in a hurry to come into my kingdom, you see, and as for John—isn't it funny to call him 'John'?—he begged me to with tears in his eyes, almost; so I promised that I would. It really doesn't matter, only when people take us for father and child, as I suppose they will, sometimes, it may shock their sense of filial respect to hear me address him as ' John' ! "

She laughed again and kissed the jewel that flashed on her hand.

" Louise !" she cried, " don't look so sober ! You shall have everything that his money will buy, and you shall live with me forever and ever in splendid style. You were made for velvets and satins and rich things in general, with that regal air of yours, and I'll fix up a whole suite of rooms for your very own."

Miss Darlington shook her head. " I couldn't, Dorris; the life you will live would stifle me !"

Her sister caught her about the waist.

" Then you'll have to 'stifle,' Sissy, for it's settled that you are to live with us, so there! I couldn't live without you, don't you see?"

CHAPTER III.

Kitty's life for the next six weeks was miserable enough to draw tears from the sympathetic.

Breakfasts went unappreciated, luncheons were sometimes completely ignored, —and dinners left untasted by her two young ladies, who were "too tired to eat."

Dorris wanted a church wedding, but the fact that the ushers would have to be elderly men, being friends of the bridegroom, caused her to relinquish her plans and content herself with the quiet house wedding her sister advocated.

The wedding gown was to be gorgeous enough to yield compensation, however, and John Dryden's gift was a diamond necklace, which outrivalled her wildest dreams of splendor.

"You are spoiling her already," Miss Darlington told him, but he shook his head and smiled.

"Did I ever tell you anything of my past life?" he asked, after a short pause, and as she answered in the negative, he continued:

"I was born in poverty. My whole youth and manhood were spent in hardest labor. I had no time, no opportunity, no money, for the joys and pleasures and beautiful things of life.

"Then I began to make my way in the world. I pressed on and up, eagerly grasping each rung of the ladder which carried me higher, supposing that when I reached the top, I should find what my soul had hungered for all through life.

"One day I woke to realize that I had gained that summit, that I was the envied of men and that I had bartered my youth in exchange. Can you understand how I felt then?

"That was ten years ago. Now I feel that I am young again! Life is once more mine! If I can not *win* love, I can *give* it, and that is the best joy, after all!"

He turned impulsively to his companion.

"It is your sister that has done this for me. All the beauty, the joyousness, the gaiety, I missed in my youth, I find realized in her. I feel through her. I delight in her light-hearted nonsense. I live again in her airy, capricious willfulness. She is the very embodiment of all the lost joys of my youth, and I love her, Louise, I love her!"

He picked up a dainty handkerchief that belonged to Dorris and fingered it lovingly. "'There's no fool like an old fool,' you know!" he murmured, shamefacedly, and Miss Darlington turned away her eyes as the bit of lace was covertly thrust into his pocket.

So the days wore away, each seemingly shorter than the last.

Dorris went about as if dancing on air. "Everything is so deliciously new," she would exclaim, and her sister found her one day, making up a bundle of her old gowns. "I'm going to give them to Kitty," she explained. "I want to get them out of my sight—I never want to see the shabby old duds again. They make me feel dreary just to look at them."

And so the wedding day dawned and the April sunlight waked the bride by kissing her eyes in a warm caress.

"Sunshine!" she cried, sitting up in bed. "That means good luck! Sissy, your doleful prophecies are scattered to the four winds. No bride that the sun shown on was ever yet known to be unhappy!"

Miss Darlington had been up before the sun, and now came in with a bunch of bride's roses in her hands.

"John sends his greetings to you," she said, laying the exquisite flowers upon the bed.

"Goose!" laughed the little bride, burying her nose among the creamy petals. "Do you know, Sissy, my only fear for

my future content lies in the dread that
John will bore me with his dreadful
devotion. I wish he would hate me, just
a little; 'twould be a new sensation!"

" Perhaps he will some day. I think *I*
should!"

Dorris looked surprised. " Why?"
she asked.

" Because such love as he gives you
deserves a better return than you are
capable of yielding."

Dorris yawned and pelted the sober
face opposite with roses.

" You're a darling old sentimental
goose!" she cried.

The day went all too fast for the many
things that had to be attended to, but at
last Dorris stood robed in her shimmer-
ing satin gown, while her sister adjusted
the veil.

A knock at the door interrupted her,
and the white-haired bridegroom came
into the room.

His eyes were dark with excitement,
and as he caught sight of the girl in her

bridal robes, his face flushed warmly.
" Oh, Dorris, you beautiful child !" he
murmured.

She nodded to him brightly. " Is it
time to go?" she asked.

"Almost, but I—I wanted to bring you
this," he stammered, drawing forth a
jewel case as he spoke. " I have always
heard that a bride should wear a star
upon her brow. It's a foolish old super-
stition ; but you will wear it, for my sake,
won't you ?"

He opened the box and took out a star
composed of pearls.

" John, you dear, please go on indulg-
ing your foolish superstitions !" cried his
bride, brushing his cheek with her lips.

" Louise, do fasten my veil with it ;
isn't it a gem !"

He stood by as the star was being
placed, and then, taking both her hands
in his, he stooped and reverently kissed
the forehead where his gift shone forth.
All through the ceremony his eyes dwelt
upon the face at his side, and whatever

Miss Darlington may have read in his look, it filled her with compassion, and she vowed within herself that she would do all that lay in her power to make his future life as happy as she could.

CHAPTER IV.

May was smiling upon the world, and Kitty stood under the budding leaves, watching for the postman.

"Shure, an' it's toime that pretty blatherskite siut anither letter. Och ! the ways o' the wourld! Miss Louise, the swate angil, stayin' quiet at home—an' that pert sparrow gettin' all the foine things under the skoi !"

Here her soliloquy was interrupted by the appearance of the blue-coated carrier.

" Good morning, Mistress Kitty. Is there anything I can do for you to-day ?"

"Shure, yis! It's a letter from me swateheart in the ould countree that I'm a pinin' fer ! she answered, with a ponderous imitation of coquetry.

" He has died, then—a little bird told me all about it, so you'd better keep your

bright eyes out for some one nearer
home."

Kitty tossed her head as she took the
letter he handed her. " Shure, an' when
. me bright eyes see what they call a man,
Mr. Postman, they'll be after keeping a
lookout fer him!" With which retort
she fled into the house, having a truly
feminine love of the last word.

Miss Darlington looked up expectantly
as Kitty brought in the letter.

" An' is it news from the little spal-
peen?" she asked.

" Yes, Kitty; she has remembered our
existence once more; she must be coming
home."

" ' You darling old duckie,'" the letter
began; " ' I suppose it has been awful
of me not to write you ! Every morning
John has asked me if I did not intend
writing you, and I have always answered
' yes,' for I have intended to, you know !
But, heavens ! the days have been so full
of new wonders and sensations !

" Fancy me, if you can, a *grande dame*,

with a maid to wait on me and nothing to do but look as pretty as I can, and allow myself to be petted and admired. John is a dear! He loads me with everything that I happen to fancy for the moment, until, alas! even the delights of possession pall on me a little. Isn't it odd that the fact of knowing I can have everything I want robs me of half the desire? You can study that out with your owl-like wisdom. It gave me an odd sensation at first, when the men I met made love to me. Don't be shocked; that's only fashionable. I find they all do it to the married women, and it isn't much fun, either. I always want to laugh at them; they are so silly! Once I did. I was in a gondola with Tom Benton, and he was so idiotically sentimental that I giggled right out! He was furious and so sulky he wouldn't talk, so I fell asleep and never woke up till we were moored at the hotel steps. I told John, but he didn't laugh as much as I expected him to.

"Well, Italy is beautiful, I suppose, but I'm tired of it now; besides, I'm crazy to return to my new grandeur, so we are coming back home; perhaps we will sail by the next steamer.

"John says you must be there in the town house to meet us, so you had better rent the old home to those people you wrote me of, for we want to find you quite settled in the big house when we come back.

"Good-bye, you darling old Sissy. I blow you a kiss across the water.

"DORRIS DRYDEN."

Miss Darlington laid down the letter. Perhaps, for John's sake, she ought to move into the "big house;" but it would be very hard to give up the little shabby, old house that had been "home" to her as long as she could remember.

She looked about the room. There was the cosy old sofa, where she used to curl up on rainy days to read impossible fairy tales, and many a childish trouble had been wept away within its wide-spread-

ing arms. Such a comfortable old sofa,
faded and worn, like the face of some
dear old friend. Would there be anything to take its place in the "big
house?" Her eyes wandered to their
mother's writing desk, old-fashioned and
battered, with notches cut in the legs,
where Dorris had played at being a
"wood-cutter" one winter's afternoon,
long ago. The mischievous little fingers
had been sharply rapped, and Miss Darlington remembered how she had con-
soled her by rolling her in the fur rug,
and playing bear.

Laddie was lying on the rug now, and
Miss Darlington dropped down beside
him, burying her face in his neck.

" We all belong together, Laddie—the
old sofa and you and I and the rest of it,
and we won't show off well in the fine,
new house; but I'm afraid we'll have to
go, Laddie, I'm afraid we'll have to go !"
And Laddie rubbed his nose against her
cheek in dumb sympathy, wondering
foolishly what made it feel so wet !

CHAPTER V.

Three busy weeks had flown by. Miss Darlington and her few personal belongings were installed in their new home, while Kitty ruled as head cook in the kitchen.

The little old house had been rented with all its shabby furniture and everything in the big house put in order for the arrival of its master and mistress.

Louise sat in the large drawing-room, trying to interest herself in a book, though her ears were listening for the sound of carriage wheels, and at last she heard them stop before the door.

A slim figure ran lightly up the steps into the out-stretched arms. "O, Sissy! It's so good to have you here. I was so afraid you wouldn't be on hand to welcome us, and oh! I'm so tired and warm!

Send my maid right up to my room; I
must have a tubbing before I eat. John?
He's coming, but he has been ill, so
Ritchie has to handle him with care.''

Miss Darlington turned to find John
Dryden painfully climbing the steps with
the help of his valet. He looked old and
tired, and her heart went out to him.

"Lean on me," she said, going to his
side. " I am so sorry you have been ill,
but we will soon have you well again,
now you are at home. I'm a famous
nurse, you know."

"Yes," he murmured, his glance search-
ing the hall. " Where did she go?"

" Dorris ?" She went to her room to
prepare for dinner. Will you rest here,
or have something served to you in your
own apartments ?"

He sighed. " I'll wait down here. It
might sadden her home-coming if I were
sick upstairs."

Miss Darlington bit her lip. " But you
really are not equal to it," she remon-
strated.

"Yes, I am," he insisted, with slight irritation, adding eagerly, "Did you see her? Did you notice how beautiful she has grown?"

"She was looking very well and extremely gay," answered Miss Darlington, rather coldly.

"That's it, 'extremely gay;' she laughs and sings and dances all day, and a good part of every night. They all admire her so much; but she is *mine*, Louise, my wife—all mine, you know!"

"Of course, she is yours; your own happy little bride," she said, soothingly, and he brightened at her words.

He scarcely touched a morsel of food at dinner, sitting with his eyes fastened upon Dorris, at the other end of the table. Once, as she glanced brightly across at him, he smiled and raised his wine glass to his lips. "To your home-coming, Mrs. John Dryden," he said.

She nodded: "It's nice to be at home at last, isn't it, John?" and the few careless words brought a flush to his cheek, which lingered long after she had forgotten the remark.

Later on, she sat on a low stool at his feet, allowing him to play with her hair as it rested against his knee, while her tongue ran on about all that she had seen and heard since she had been away.

"I liked Paris best of all," she declared. "There were a lot of artists there; funny people who lived in scrubby rooms. John ran across the son of one of his old friends, who was one of these amusing creatures, so he took us right into the midst of their queer life. It was perfect Bohemia, and I used to enjoy going to his studio. He painted my picture, too—don't twitch my hair so, John!"

Louise glanced at his face and was struck at the change she saw in it. Dorris moved her head from beneath his touch and continued her chatter.

"He did it superbly! I sat to him in my wedding gown, you know, and John wanted to buy the picture from him, but he would not sell it. He called it his 'inspiration.' Odd that he wouldn't sell it, I think, for he appears to be awfully poor."

"John is ill!" suddenly exclaimed Louise, springing towards him.

He shook his head. "Only tired," he murmured. "If you'll ring for Ritchie, I'll go to my room."

His face looked white and drawn, but Dorris called forth a shadowy smile by drawing his head against her breast and lightly touching her lips to his brow.

"Too bad!" she said. "You're all tired out. You ought to have gone straight to bed as soon as you got here."

He did not reply, save by the look of devotion that lay in his eyes as they rested upon her face, and she stood at his side, running her fingers through his whitened hair, until the valet appeared to take him to his room.

"Why didn't you go with him?" asked Miss Darlington, as the door closed.

"Go with him? Why on earth should I?

Ritchie is paid to take care of him, and he does it all right."

Dorris lounged over to the window. "It's a heavenly night," she went on. "I wish something nice would happen, somebody awfully interesting come, or an exciting bit of news blow in to us."

"Still longing for sensations? I should think even you would be satisfied with the new experiences of the last few months."

Dorris shook her head, yawning. "Everything gets to be a bore if you have all you want of it. Not that I would go back to the old days in that shabby little house of ours—ugh! it makes me ill just to think of those days. I don't see how I existed then. Imagine me, now, wearing a gown that I had 'made over' myself on that rheumatic old machine—stitch, stitch, stitch, clack, clack, clack—horrors! It's much pleas- anter to be bored as I am!"

Miss Darlington laughed. "You are nothing but a child," she said; "always in search of new toys. What will it be next?"

"The seaside! I'm going there in a few days."

"I don't think John is strong enough," objected her sister.

"Well, we can leave him here, then."

"What! desert that poor old man, whose very sun sets when you are away from him?"

"O, don't be a prig, Louise! I shan't 'desert' him, but I can't be tied to him all summer long."

"If you go, you'll go alone. I shall stay with John!"

Dorris lost her temper. "You act as if he were your husband!" she cried.

"If he were, I should do my duty towards him!" was the quick reply.

"Duty! duty! duty! What a bugbear you make of that word! I *do* do my 'duty' when I am pleasant and agreeable to him. Didn't you see how I rubbed his head and kissed him to-night?"

Miss Darlington looked at her sister as

she lay stretched full length among the cushions of the couch.

" You are incorrigible !" she sighed.

"Don't preach, Sissy ; it does bore me so. I endured it as Dorris Darlington, but as Mrs. John Dryden—I *won't!*"

A pause followed her words. "You won't go to the shore with me, then?" she asked, at last.

" No !"

"Then don't. Mrs. Nettleton will be glad to have me at her cottage."

No answer was made to this announcement, but Miss Darlington rose and folded her embroidery.

Dorris watched her until she had reached the door, then she sprang up and ran after her.

"O, you dear, sanctimonious old Sissy," she cried, squeezing her. "Kiss me good-night, quick, or I'll cry. You mustn't scold me ; it doesn't agree with me !"

Her sister melted—she always did when those clinging arms were about her neck, and she gave the kiss as they went up-stairs together.

"I don't approve of you, though, Dorris," she said, but young Mrs. John ran away laughing, with her hands held over her ears.

CHAPTER VI.

As Miss Darlington had expected, John Dryden made an attempt to accompany his wife to the seaside ; but after spending two days there, he was forced to return to the quiet of his own home, leaving young Mrs. Dryden at her friend's cottage.

The parting was hard for him, and Miss Darlington's heart ached sympathetically as she watched the sadness grow in his face, as every mile bore him further and further from the sunshine of his life.

She redoubled her attentions, and felt rewarded when, after reaching home, he looked up at her and told her it was good to have her with him.

" Why did you come back with the old man, instead of staying on there to enjoy yourself?"

"I wanted to come," she assured him. "It is much nicer here than at that crowded hotel, and we will have a cosy time of it, all by ourselves."

She read to him until he fell asleep from utter weariness, then leaning back in her chair she gave herself up to dreams.

How strange this new life was; this new world of ease and luxury, which seemed so oddly unreal after the years she had spent in fighting with stern realities. Would she ever feel at home amid all this stifling grandeur? Her thoughts went back to the dear famíliarity of the old house. It may have been shabby, but it was hers! It had grown to be part of her, and home is where the heart is, surely.

"Nothing is worth anything without love!"

The sound of her own voice startled her, or was it the step behind which she had not heard before?

Turning quickly, she came face to face with a young man, in whose eyes she read an open amusement, which showed he had overheard her soliloquy. Her color rose.

"I am Mr. Dryden's secretary," he explained, coming to her relief. "He sent for me, but I see he is now otherwise engaged."

They both smiled, as a slight snore testified to the soundness of the sleep enjoyed by the old man.

"He was very tired; would you mind waiting? I can't bear to disturb him," she pleaded.

The young man seated himself. "Mr. Dryden is not very strong; he has been such a hard worker all his life," he said.

"Yes," she answered. "He has spent his life in accumulating wealth, and now he finds he can't eat it, nor warm his heart with it, nor buy love with it!"

Her companion looked at her in sudden surprise.

"I beg pardon, but—er—aren't you Mrs. John Dryden?"

" Good heavens, no !" she cried. "How could you suppose such a thing?"

Her indignation brought a flush to his face.

" I have never seen his wife," he murmured apologetically.

She flushed in her turn.

" Of course not. I forgot that. Please pardon my annoyance at the mistake, but it gave me a sort of shock to think any one could fancy *I* would marry him, you know."

He read more than she intended in her words.

" I understand," he said simply, while she went on to explain her sister's absence as best she might.

The clock ticked away the moments while they talked, and still John Dryden slept.

Miss Darlington learned that her new friend's name was Leigh Kurt and that he had been Mr. Dryden's secretary for several years   He told her a great deal about the old man's character that warmed her heart and she found that his hard-earned money was not spent selfishly, but that his charities were broad and far-reaching.

"He deserves to be happy in his old age. I was glad when he told me of his marriage to your sister; it seemed to make him young again."

As if the mention of her name brought the dreamer back to earth, he opened his eyes and looked about with the dazed expression of one newly awakened.

" Asleep, eh? and you let me snooze while you two sat and laughed at my snoring, I suppose!"

He put out his hand to Kurt. " Well, I don't begrudge you the laugh, for I have had the best nap I can remember for weeks. Now we will begin on the work, Leigh, my boy."

For two hours he kept his secretary busy, and then, tired out, he was carried away by the faithful Ritchie, leaving instructions for Kurt to stay to dinner and keep Miss Darlington from being lonely.

And so they talked. It seemed as though they had been treasuring thoughts all their lives before, just for this wonderful meeting, and when eleven o'clock chimed from the big hall clock, they parted with the feeling that they had known each other not moments, nor hours, but from the earliest birth of their souls.

Who can tell what it is that draws two spirits into this close communion, leaving an impress which a lifetime cannot efface?

Only eternity can answer!

CHAPTER VII.

Dorris sat writing her first letter to her husband. Louise had sent another long, tiresome epistle to her, filled with quotations from the Bible about the duty of wives to their husbands, and so, chiefly to prevent a repetition of the lecture, she had left the gay group of loungers below and ascended to her room to accomplish the task demanded of her.

The soft sea breezes fanned her cheek, lifting the hair from her forehead and lulling her into a state of idle content.

For a long time she sat nibbling her pen and gazing out upon the sparkling water, watching the white sea gulls skim over its placid depths, like pure thoughts hovering over a calmly peaceful heart. Then she was seized with an inspiration and began to write rapidly.

" 'Dearest of dear Husbands,' " she commenced. She knew it would please him to have her address him so.

" 'I have been thinking of you so much that I could not put off writing you a day longer. You see, I am kept so very busy that it is almost impossible to find time for anything, but this morning I have run away from everyone just to write you a letter. Louise tells me you are feeling better, and you know how happy that makes your wife feel, don't you?" She smiled as she wrote the word " wife," underscoring it twice.

" 'I am having a very jolly time of it, down here. Mrs. Nettleton wants to take me into the mountains for a little run, and I think I will go with her, unless you write me not to do so ; but I know you don't need me when you have good old Sissy to take care of you. She is just the most comforting thing in all the world, you know !

" By the way, she forwarded me a letter from Allan. He writes he is com-

ing over soon, and says he exhibited my
picture and it has brought him fame.
I'm hugely flattered. It's a new sensation to feel all Paris is raving over me—
or is it my gown? Anyway, you are
awfully proud of me. Aren't you?

"Tell Louise she musn't cut me out
too completely. I'm half inclined to be
jealous of your devotion to her, you
know.

"And now, au revoir, my dearest
husband, with the devoted love of your
'wee wifie,'   DORRIS DRYDEN."

She stamped and addressed this epistle
with a pleased smile. "It is rather pleasant to do one's duty; Sissy is right,"
she thought, running down stairs, "only
I don't think I could stand very much
of it!"

"Where art thou going, my pretty
maid?"

"Oh! Mr. Preston! You startled me
awfully! I wish you would stop pounc-
ing upon me like that! It bores me! I
feel as if I were haunted!"

"You liked to be 'bored,' at first!"
he said, reproachfully.

"Perhaps! It was a new sensation,
then."   .

"You don't seem to care for anything
but experiencing 'new sensations,'" he
replied, sulkily. "Some day there is
bound to be an end. There is nothing
really 'new' under the sun. Then what
will you do?"

"I'll wait till that time comes. It
seems pretty far off at present."

"It will come, though," he persisted,
"and then you will probably be a blase
old woman, with no one to fetch and
carry for you as I do!"

She raised her eyes to his in a swift
glance. "Where will you be then?"
she murmured softly.

He groaned, "At your feet still, I suppose. I am, as you say, a fool!"

She nodded.

"Exactly. Now run and post this letter
for me, please."

He took it from her hand, reading the
address with cynically raised eyebrows.

She answered his glance with a laugh.
"Go!" she cried. "It is a love letter
and must catch the early mail."

"Will you wait here till I come back?"
he asked.

She nodded.

"Promise!" he insisted.

"I promise. Hurry!"

He turned and walked rapidly away,
but when the trees hid him from sight,
she caught up her skirts and ran in the
opposite direction as fast as her feet
would carry her.

CHAPTER VIII.

A week later, Dorris found herself in danger of becoming bored.

The weather was too warm for exertion, and the days seemed endlessly long and dull.

"I never thought it could be so stifling," she exclaimed.

Someone yawned audibly, but no other response greeted her remark.

"I never knew that people could be so stupid; it makes me sleepy just to look at you all."

"It's too beastly hot for anything but the necessary breathing we are obliged to do," spoke up a voice at her side.

"The evenings are cool enough. Why not go on an all-night picnic?" Dorris suggested.

"It wouldn't be proper," put in her friend and hostess.

"But it would be perfectly lovely! We'll go on Mr. Preston's yacht, and sail and sail, sail and sail, till the moon goes down. 'Twill be deliciously cool. I'm going. Who'll go with me?"

No one promised; but when the moon rose that night it blushed to see that a party of rash young people had started out alone under its luring rays.

Over the silvered, rippling waters the little yacht skimmed, bearing them far away from all conventional restrictions, and filling them with reckless delight. It seemed almost as much fun as if they were running away from school.

Gradually the laughter subsided, and a dreamy quiet fell upon them all. On and on they sailed, following the moonbeams' glittering pathway, lulled by the gentle cradling of the waves. Dorris grew sleepy.

"Do talk," she exclaimed, turning to Preston. "What have you been thinking about for the last half hour?"

" Of a little poem I ran across the other day," he answered, softly.

" What was it?"

" Shall I repeat it?"

" If you choose."

He let his eyes rest upon her face as he repeated the lines :

" 'Tother day, as I was twining
Roses for her crown to dine in,
What, of all things, midst the heap,
Should I light on, fast asleep,
But the little desperate elf—
That tiny traitor—Love, himself !
By the wings I pinched him up
Like a bee, and in a cup
Of wine I plunged and sank him.
And what d'you think I did ? I *drank* him !
Faith ! I thought him dead—not he !
For there he lives in ten-fold glee,
And now, this moment, with his wings
I feel him tickling my heart strings !' "

She laughed. " Don't you think it is a *mosquito* you feel 'tickling'? I saw a big one vanish into your mouth just a moment ago !"

He turned away from her. " I might

have expected a laugh from you—you
jeer at everything !"

Some one called across the boat : " I
say, Preston, the wind is dropping off
considerably ; think there is danger of a
calm ? "

Long streaks of grey could be seen,
faintly heralding the dawn.   The moon
had warned them of the flight of time by
dropping into the edge of the sea, and
now the breezes seemed to be fainting at
the approach of day.

" We are making the best time we
can," Preston replied, rising to scan the
horizon ; but the land seemed to recede
as the darkness faded into the rosy-tinted
light.

They sat huddled together in the chilly
air—a cheerless, bedraggled-looking set
of people.

Dorris began to laugh.   " We will get
in just in time to meet everyone," she
cried.

"It's all your fault !   You made us

come," declared a tearful voice ; and, for once, young Mrs. Dryden made no reply.

The yacht could be plainly seen from the shore, rocking helplessly upon the tide.

Signs of life began to show and knots of people gathered to gaze at them through field-glasses. At last a launch was sent out to tow them in, and the culprits were forced to run the gauntlet of the curious and the shocked.

Dorris received a new sensation as she passed the different groups of acquaintances, who stared at her in haughty disapproval; but she held her head so high that censure fell upon her more heavily than it otherwise might have done, and when she reached her friend's cottage, that lady gave her such a generous piece of her mind, that the afternoon found young Mrs. John Dryden steaming back to the city.

CHAPTER IX.

It was dusk when the cab drew up before her own door and she ran eagerly up the steps and into the drawing-room.

A picture of home greeted her eyes. John Dryden leaned back in a large easy chair, listening to the young man who was reading aloud, while Miss Darlington sat under the yellow lamp rays, embroidering some dainty article.

"I've come home!" she cried.

They all sprang to their feet in amazement.

"Dorris! what has brought you back so unexpectedly?" exclaimed her sister, while John Dryden drew her to him in joy too deep for words.

"O, I got tired of them all down there, so I came home. Aren't you all awfully glad to see me?"

It was unnecessary to ask that of the gray-haired man, whose eager eyes devoured her face, and, as she slipped into her old seat at his feet, he laid his hand upon her head with the tenderness a mother might show for a wayward child.

Leigh Kurt was introduced after the surprise of her arrival had subsided, and she was not long in discovering some subtle change in her sister, which puzzled her at first. But her quick eyes saw many things, as she sat, chattering, in their midst, and, that night, after every one had gone to their rooms, Miss Darlington was surprised by receiving a visit from her sister.

" Don't disturb yourself," she said, slipping into a low seat. " I have tucked John into bed, and now I have come here to perform another duty."

"You are developing a marvelous aptitude for duty!" laughed the other.

Dorris nodded.   " I am alarmed at what I saw to-night, you see, and I have come to point out to you the error of your ways."

Miss Darlington turned from the dressing table, letting her heavy hair fall from her hands.

" Dorris, what are you talking about ?"

" Don't look so innocent, my love ; you're a great fraud. Here you have lectured me all my life, but I never did anything so reprehensible as to flirt with a young and unsuspecting youth, who"—

"Hush ! " cried Miss Darlington, her face hot with blushes. "You don't know what you are talking about, child !"

Dorris read the face before her in sudden consternation. " You don't mean to say you are in *earnest?* Oh, Sissy, Sissy !"

" Why shouldn't I be?" asked her sister, trying to hide her flushed face behind her unbound hair.

" Why? Why, because you have only known him a few weeks, and oh, Sissy, he is POOR ! "

Louise Darlington looked down at the little figure crouching upon the low seat.

"Dorris," she said, and Dorris thrilled strangely at the sweet note in her voice, "I loved him the first time we met. I believe I shall love him through life and the mysteries that come after life. I think I must have loved him in some previous existence which only our two souls shared. As for his poverty—ah, child! you can't understand me when I say that it adds a joy to my love to know that I shall serve him—that I shall help to bear the burdens that are his!"

Silence fell between them as Miss Darlington ceased speaking.

Dorris gazed at her in awed wonder.

"Don't look at me like that, dear; can't you tell me you are glad because of my—my happiness?"

Dorris rose slowly. putting her arms about her sister: "I'm glad—you are so glad!" she began, lamely, and then, with a burst of unexpected feeling, she cried: "But oh, Sissy, you will have to go away from me, and what shall I do without you? What can I do with John?"

Miss Darlington gathered the small form closer to her, kissing the bowed head.

"I couldn't live here forever, sweetheart," she whispered. "You will have to bear the responsibility of your marriage some day, so I promised Leigh I would be his wife early in October."

Dorris sobbed : "Oh, dear, what shall I do?"

" You will be a woman, Dorris, and do your duty as a wife," answered her sister, firmly. "You married John with open eyes, and you must abide by the consequences."

The slight form wriggled in the other's arms. "Don't preach," she mumbled, through her tears.

An irrepressible smile flitted over Miss Darlington's face.

" Aren't you ever going to grow up?" she asked.

Dorris withdrew herself and dried her eyes. "I suppose I'll have to if I've got to be John's wife all alone !" she sighed.

"I always thought you would stay with me forever, and you always see that everything goes right."

Miss Darlington laughed in what seemed to be a most heartless manner.

"You've deserted me utterly!" cried her sister, "and I really believe you think it is John who has been 'sacrificed' by our marriage, instead of me!"

"I'm afraid I do, Dorris," was the grave reply. Before your marriage I felt as though you were selling your womanhood, your youth, but now I fear his happiness was the price he paid for you!"

"Well, he would have me!" retorted Dorris, petulantly, and then she drew a long sigh. "Oh, Sissy, if I could only be as good and splendid as you are. You look so happy to-night, happier with your prospect of a life of mean economies before you, than *I* am with all my money and the world at my feet! Why are we so different? I couldn't be happy if I were to be poor again, you know!"

"Not even with love?" asked her sister, softly.

Dorris shook her head, turning slowly away.

"No, not even with love!" she answered drearily, as she left the room.

CHAPTER X.

September and October had passed, and November held full sway.

Flowers lay withered by the chilly kiss of frost, while the trees, disrobing, blushed at the freedom of the winds.

Miss Darlington had been Mrs. Leigh Kurt for over a month, and Dorris found life a very difficult thing. John had made no demands upon her, but the look in Sissy's eyes when she kissed her good-bye had haunted her ever since, and compelled her to exert herself for his amusement with unwonted zeal

To judge from his appearance as he sat at the breakfast table, overlooking the mail, he had thriven upon this new treatment.

" Two letters for Mrs. John Dryden," he said, handing them across to her. " One is from Louise, isn't it?"

" Yes, and the other from Allan Kip."

She did not see his brow cloud at that name, for she had opened the letter and was reading its contents eagerly.

" He is coming at last!" she cried. " He says he may drop down on us at any time, and brings his new found fame to share with me, because it was my picture that first brought it to him."

She laughed, beginning to re-read portions of the letter.

" Have you forgotten your letter from Louise?"

She started at his tone. "Of course not," she replied, flushing slightly as she glanced at his face, and slipping the other missive into her pocket.

" Dear old Sissy! I wonder if she is still in Paradise?"

Mrs. Kurt's letter was long and closely written.

" ' Summer has not yet left us,' " she wrote.

" Of course not," sighed Dorris. " She and Leigh would think it was summer as long as they could gaze into each other's eyes."

" ' And we are enjoying each moment in this wonderful climate. It seems like the sweet old story of the Garden of Eden that Leigh and I are living over again, only that the serpent is happily absent.

" ' I never knew such content was possible for mortals to taste. It is so wonderful to be always with him. We walk together, and read, and sing, and talk. Oh, it's marvelous how much we have to talk over.

" ' And then, in the twilight we draw close to each other ' "——

Dorris broke off abruptly. " This is positively worse than any dime novel I ever read," she exclaimed. " Sissy is old enough to know better. It makes me ill to read such stuff."

She tossed the letter to her husband and rose from her seat.

His eyes followed her wistfully, but

he did not speak, and she stood at the window while he finished the letter.

Suddenly the door opened and a young man sprang to meet her with outstretched hands.

" Allan !" she cried.

He kissed her hands with a foreign grace that suited him well, and turned to John Dryden.

"I wanted to surprise you," he laughed.

The old man looked at him as he stood talking to Dorris.   How young and handsome he was, with the fire of genius in his great dark eyes, and how bright her face appeared as she lifted it to his. He watched the color come and go in her cheeks, feeling suddenly very old and tired—so tired !

After this the days flew by on bright-hued wings for young Mrs. Dryden.

All the time Allan could spare from his painting, he spent at her side, and no one seemed to notice that the light had left John Dryden's face, giving place to a patient resignation which held an epitome of pathos. No one observed that he shrank more and more within himself as the winter rolled by, until it was a rare thing to find him in the drawing-room, or anywhere but in his own apartments.

Dorris was in her element. As the privileged friend of society's new idol, she reigned supreme, and she gave a series of teas, at which she received with Allan by her side, clad in his most picturesque garb, and with the dreamy look in his beautiful eyes which caused the women to flutter about him like a flock of enamored doves.

And so the snow fell, hiding the earth's worn and scarred face with its virginal veil of purity, and Mr. and Mrs. Kurt returned to settle down in their cosy little home.

Dorris still went to " Sissy " when in need of comfort, and was always glad to have her come to the "big house," for her visits brightened John and chased away that reproachful expression in his eyes which annoyed her so that she avoided him as much as possible.

Mrs. Kurt had been shocked at the change she found in him, but she soon discovered that remonstrance was useless.

Leigh was indignant. "Your sister is killing him by her heartlessness," he said to her one day. "He was only lonely before his marriage, but now he is wretched."

There was another anxietythat weighed upon her which she dared not mention, even to Leigh. It had haunted her ever since she had surprised Dorris and Allan in the music room one afternoon. Their start at her sudden entrance, the hot flush in her sister's averted face, told her more than she cared to know and filled her with forebodings.

All through the winter she watched and prayed with a dull despair gnawing at her heart, wondering what the end would be.

CHAPTER XI.

"Sissy! Sissy! Where are you? One would think it an easy task to find you in such a box of a house as this. Well, now you are happy, I suppose!"

Young Mrs. John paused on the threshold of the kitchen, holding aside her silken skirts with one gloved hand, as she surveyed the scene before her.

" Mrs. Kurt was on her knees before the stove, while an appearance of general disorder prevailed.

She let her hands fall in her lap, as she looked up at her sister with a twinkle in her eyes.

" Don't despise poor Cinderella, my haughty sister," she cried, the twinkle broadening into a laugh, as the contrast between them was borne in upon her.

" I am not always like this, but acci-

dents will happen, and this morning
Judith burned her hand and had to go
home for a week's rest, and *I* haven't the
slightest idea how to make this stove
work. All the dampers seem invented
to extinguish the fire, no matter how I
may arrange them. Can't you give me
an idea how to manage it?"

"Heavens, no!" exclaimed Dorris,
stepping gingerly across the floor and
perching herself upon a corner of the
kitchen table.

"Do get up and wash your hands,
Louise. It's disgraceful for you to look
like that. I can't see how you can be
happy living in such a stuffy sort of
way."

Mrs. Kurt laughed; her eyes were
sparkling, and Dorris thought she had
never seen her look so bright and pretty.

"I love it!" she cried, rising to do as
her sister asked. "Every inch of this
snug little nest is dear to me, and I would
rather have it than all your grandeur. It
is a *home* I want—not a palace."

Young Mrs. Dryden looked about the tiny kitchen disdainfully, but the other only laughed.

> " 'Disdain, Thou art the brightest,
> The daintiest, the lightest
> Of all the sins of Earth,' "

she quoted gaily.

" Come, Dorris, let me and my peculiar tastes pass by, and tell me what has brought you over this morning.   Is John ill?"

" Of course not! Why should he be? He takes most awfully good care of his health.   I just came over because I was bored with everything and I wanted a change of air."

" Well, you got it, but it doesn't seem to agree with you. Take off your hat and stay till Leigh comes home. We'll have to have a cold lunch, because I can't make the stove work, but you won't mind that, for you feast every day in the year."

Dorris watched her sister bustling cheerily about her little domain, setting the table with deftness, cutting thin

slices of creamy-looking bread and bringing out home-made preserves with a
proud and house-wifely smile.

" I'm always wishing to myself that I
could be like you, Sissy," she said at last,
but the opening of the front door pre-
vented Mrs. Kurt's reply, as she ran out
into the hall to meet her husband.

Dorris still perched upon the table,
heard the sound of smothered caresses,
intermingled with low-toned, tender murmurings.

Idiots! " she ejaculated, feeling in
some way personally aggrieved as they
came in with smiling lips and joy-kissed
eyes.

They sat down to the luncheon which,
though daintily served, smacked of an
economy that was too suggestive of by-
gone days to give her any real enjoy-
ment.

Yet how gay "Sissy" seemed. She
and Leigh were like two children playing
" tea party." They laughed over the
simplest joke with a heartiness that made

her marvel, and when Leigh was sent to
replenish the sugar bowl, bringing it back
filled with salt, how they did laugh over
the mistake.

After lunch Leigh donned a big check
apron and pretended to help clear the
table, but after dropping the best cut-
glass dish he was turned out, covered
with disgrace and—kisses.

" I think I will go, too," Dorris yawned.

" Do we bore you?"

" Yes—a little. You are so abominably
happy. I feel as if I had eaten lunch in
a candy shop."

Her sister laughed, though her eyes
dwelt upon the face opposite with tender
regret. " I'm sorry you can't be ' abominably happy,' too," she said. " Where
are you going now?"

" To the ' Zoo.' It's quite the fad to
go to the Gardens this year, and I have
fallen in love with a great white bear,
who is as tame as a kitten and lets me
feed and pet him all I wish. His trainer

has taught him to dance the minuette on his hind legs, and he does it adorably."

Mrs. Kurt stood on the little porch watching the vanishing vision of bright silks and floating laces.

" Poor little Dorris!" she sighed. " Poor, poor John ! "

She lifted her eyes to the white floating clouds above, letting her fancies drift idly along with them.

The soft spring air touched her forehead like a kiss of Hope, and the twittering of two domesticated birds told her that summer was near. What was this mysterious promise that the spring always held, filling every heart with subtle bliss, with the feeling that joy was coming, coming, coming?

Each springtide, in the scorching heat of summer, died ; always the chilly winter winds chased away the birds, covering old earth with ice and snow once more. Yet still the springtime brought back its mystic joy to hearts, and flowers burst into bloom as if Death was but a forgotten fancy.

A bright-eyed bird hopped to her feet in happy trust ; a bursting bud on the vine above brushed her cheek, and a soft breeze stole to her as if it were a message of love from the arching Heavens.

" Ah !" she cried, in sudden ecstacy. " It is a foretaste of eternal joy which comes to us in this brief season of Promise ! Spring is the Easter of our hearts, in its sweetness we taste the bliss that is to come."

CHAPTER XII.

A week later the quiet street resounded to the steel-clad hoofs of two well groomed horses, and curious neighbors ran to their windows to watch as the handsome turn-out stopped before Mrs. Leigh Kurt's modest home.

Dorris had sent a note to her sister :

"I'm going to give a ball and I'm awfully busy, but John is ill, and thinks I ought to stay at home and nurse him. Do come and cheer him up and give me a chance to do a few of the hundred things necessary. I'm going to have a surprise that will be the sensation of the season, but even you aren't to know of it 'till the night of the ball. It's a grand secret! Come take care of John for me to-day. Do !"

Mrs. Kurt wondered what her sister had in her head this time, but when she reached the house she found John so feverish and sick that everything else went out of her mind.

She tried to sooth him by reading aloud, but he begged her to stop, saying he would rather talk. She laid aside the book and took up her embroidery, but he only lay looking at her with dim, saddened eyes.

At last she began to speak of the ball and the secret Dorris treasured, and at the mention of that name he broke in a fit of weeping that startled her out of her usual self-possession.

"Oh, don't, don't," she cried, running to him. " It is so dreadful to hear you cry like this. What is the trouble? Won't you tell me? Won't you let me help you?"

" I am so old, so old," he sobbed, " and I am dying, Louise. I shall have to go away and leave her—my beautiful Dorris ! She will be glad to have me go, too. She will welcome freedom, and then she will marry some young lover and forget me. Forget me—the troublesome old man, who tires her with his devotion. Oh, I love her so, Louise, with all the arder of youth, with all the depth of age !"

Mrs. Kurt could find nothing to say in the face of this misery. She had warned him in the old days, but he had not listened, and now he must bear his pain alone.

As if reading her thought he cried :

" But I am glad I made her my wife. She is mine, mine, mine, and I have had hours of bliss that is worth the misery. You mustn't blame her, Louise. You are a good woman, and all good women are hard sometimes, but you mustn't blame my Dorris too harshly, She is so bright, so winsome, so gay and young, it is not her fault that she can not bear to be tied to this shrunken body. But, oh, if only she could see my heart—how young it is —how full of passionate love for her! But she can't, she can't. There is no help for me, no help, no help."

He lay among the pillows and groaned aloud.

His companion knelt beside him full of unspoken sympathy, and gradually the storm spent itself, leaving him shaken and weak.

"You are very patient with the old man," he murmured, looking up into her face with an effort to smile.

For answer she stooped and kissed him.

Leigh came in as the daylight faded, and they sat talking together in the gathering twilight until the regular breathing from the couch told them the old man had fallen asleep, and they stole quietly out, leaving him alone in the midst of the creeping shadows of the night.

CHAPTER XIII.

When Mr. and Mrs. Kurt reached the big house on the night of the ball, they found it ablaze with light. The air was heavy with the scent of flowers and guests were arriving in a continuous stream.

"Where is John?" Louise asked, meeting Dorris on the stairs.

"He isn't well enough to come down. Isn't my gown lovely, Sissy? It's a sensation in itself!" She passed on as she spoke, and her sister turned towards John's room.

All was dim and quiet in that far-off nook, and the master of the house lay back among his pillows with weary, sleepless eyes staring into the gloom.

"It is like you to come to the old man," he said, holding her hands in his and gently patting them. "Did you see Dorris? She looks like a lily—a beautiful, pure, Easter lily. When she came to see me before going downstairs, it seemed as if summer had come back to me! Her face was like the wild roses I used to gather in the country years ago. But it was a dream, Louise. I am only an old man, up here alone in the dark, while all the world makes merry and forgets me!"

"Not all the world, dear."

"No, you are one of the faithful. But you must go now, she opens the ball at ten. Goodnight, don't let the memory of me spoil your pleasure. I must surely go to sleep soon, now, and it has done me good to see you. Tell Leigh he has the sweetest woman on earth for his wife."

She turned away regretfully, feeling out of the mood for the gay scene below.

Leigh was waiting for her downstairs.

"Dorris has outdone herself," he said. " Every one " was there. The bril-

liantly lighted rooms thronged with men
and women whose names stood high in
the social scale, and all were alike curious
to know what new eccentricity Mrs.
Dryden was about to commit.

At last the opening bars of the minuette were played by the flower-screened
orchestra, and the heavy curtains at the
end of the room were drawn back, dis-
closing a scene which electrified the company.

Dorris stood facing them, clad in her
picturesque gown of white ; she held her
head high, and her eyes were dark with
excitement.   With one hand she brushed
aside the draperies and the other rested
lightly upon the neck of a large white
bear, who stood upon his hind legs at her
side, gravely gazing at the throng of
richly dressed people out of his greedy
little eyes.

Confusion reigned ! Dignified chaperones screamed, nervous girls fainted
and men backed against the walls endeav-

oring not to show their fear to the fashionable world.

Mrs. Kurt stood as if turned to stone, but Allan Kip sprang forward in horror.

Dorris waved him aside with an imperative gesture, advancing to the center of the room beside her burly escort.

Together they began to bow and turn in the stately figures of the dance. Perfectly in time kept Bruin, turning and twisting, bowing and swaying as gracefully as any old spark of the old regime, and Dorris smiled upon him with all the witchery of coquettish womanhood.

The guests looked on in speechless amazement. A breathless silence had fallen upon all. The indescribable charm of the weird, ever-changing picture fascinated them, and gradually the first shock of terror subsided, as they gazed in spellbound wonder.

To and fro, up and back, moved the two white forms, swaying rythmically to the melting music. The clumsily graceful animal leading the slender and wil-

lowy woman,—was ever such a sight wit-
nessed in a ballroom before?

Allan's face was white, and the eyes
following every movement of the dancers
were filled with suppressed fire.

At last the pantomime came to an end;
the orchestra drew one long, sweet, final
note, and sir Bruin came to a halt, standing erect and sedate, gazing waggishly
over his shoulder at the assembled guests.

Every one drew a sigh of relief as the
curtains fell behind his majestic form.

" Well, I never! This is quite too
much for me!" cried one old lady, de-
scending from a chair that she had
mounted in her first fright. " Mrs. John
Dryden may think she has been funny,
but she has gone too far, this time!"

A tall spinster turned to the girl she
chaperoned. " I'm going to take you
home!" she said.

Nevertheless, there were plenty to
crowd about Dorris with exclamations of
amazement and admiration.

"How did you happen to think of it," cried one girl.

"I was so frightened at first, I thought he would jump over every one and eat me up!" put in another.

"Dorris laughed. "Why should he eat you, if he left me untouched? He is as tame as a cat; I know him well!"

"How did you happen to meet your new friend?" asked a young man near by.

"I was properly introduced by his keeper at the 'Zoo !' " she answered. "He used to watch for me (and the cakes I always took him) and one day, when his trainer made him dance the minuette, I conceived this brilliant idea, just to vary the monotony of the ball, you know!"

" You certainly succeeded, "broke in her sister's voice, "but I'm afraid you have made enemies by your absurdity."

" Don't call it an ' absurdity,' Mrs. Kurt, I think I never saw so charming a sight in my life. It was a beautiful illustration of ' Beauty and the Beast.' "

Dorris rewarded the speaker with a smile, promising him the honor of being her next partner.

Late in the evening Allan came to her. "Will you give me this dance?" he asked.

She looked up at him : "I don't know whether I will or not!" she answered. "You look as if you might be very disagreeable and cross!"

For answer, he put his arm around her, and drew her in among the dancers. He took only a few turns, stopping before a small room called "the den," which had not been thrown open to the guests that night.

He closed the door behind them and turned to face her. She shrank back.

"What makes you look so strangely?" she whispered.

" Dorris!" he cried, "have I placed you upon a pedestal that is too high for you? Do I only imagine the beauty of soul which I have ascribed to you? Are

you the tender child I think, or only a
vain and empty woman of the world?"

"Dorris fidgeted. "What have I done
to be so scolded?"

" Done!" he exclaimed. "You have
made yourself conspicuous in the most
ridiculous way, to-night. You have
offended hundreds of your friends, and
made your name a synonym for rapid dare
deviltry, bad taste and unwomanliness!
And I have to stand aside, helpless to
shield you—I, who love you so, oh,
child!"

She stood before him trembling and
clasping her fingers nervously.

He looked down at her. "I'm sorry,
Allan! I only thought what fun it would
be to surprise and scare them all. I knew
it would make such a sensation."

He groaned inwardly, but his eyes
softened in spite of himself, and she, seeing this, drew closer to him, lifting her
face to his.

"Allan!" she whispered, "did you
mean—the other?"

He caught her in his arms. "You know I did!" he cried, passionately. "I have loved you always!"

CHAPTER XIV.

Lent had come and society indulged only in afternoon teas, where religious arguments gave a fitting tone to the conversation.

John Dryden had become a confirmed invalid, and Dorris begged her sister to stay with her for his sake, an argument which prevailed upon Mrs. Kurt to close her own little home and move up into the big house, temporarily.

She herself felt convinced that it would not be necessarily long, though no one else seemed to realize that John Dryden's life was ebbing away.

"What has become of Allan Kip?" she asked, one day, as she and Dorris sat busy with their sewing in John's room.

Young Mrs. Dryden's head bent lower over her work. "He has gone away,"

she answered at last in a half-smothered
voice ; and though nothing more was
said, she rose and slipped out of the room
soon after.

The days dragged slowly by, dull,
leaden-hued and dreary.

Dorris was listless, or pitifully gay,
and she escaped from her sister's search-
ing eyes as often as possible. John's
strength failed daily, but she would not
see it, and spent as little of her time in
his room as she could.

The nursing came upon Mrs. Kurt, but
she silenced Leigh's objections by saying
that it comforted her to do all she could
for the dying man.

The end came, one evening, as she sat
alone with him in the twilight. He had
been more than usually restless that day,
and she was tired and worn out.

He fell into a stupor, at last, and she
listened to his heavy breathing with a
feeling of relief. Suddenly he called to
her in a strong, clear voice, and she ran

to the bedside to find him sitting up without the support of his pillows.

"Louise!" he cried, "I see everything new. I have been thinking of what I must leave. Now I see to what I am going. Oh, the joy of it! Worth all the pain! and 'He shall wipe all tears away' —all tears—all tears awa——"

The words died in a low murmur. His face caught the light of some wondrous, reflected glory, and he smiled radiantly as his spirit winged itself free.

She stood with clasped hands, thrilled by that low, rapturous cry; vaguely yearning to follow his soul in its blissful flight, and watching the glory slowly fade from the stiffening features, leaving them vacant and frozen under the touch of Death.

A light laugh floated up from below.

John Dryden was dead—and Dorris was free. What would she do with her freedom?

Her soul turned from its heavenly yearnings with a shock of pain. Nearer and nearer came the sound; careless, charming the laugh that had made all the music of the dead man's life.

The door opened : " Is John awake? I want to show him——"

The words ended in a cry of abject terror, and Mrs. Kurt caught the little figure as it swayed backwards.

" Hush!" she said, feeling almost as if the cry might waken the peaceful sleeper.

" He was glad to go, Dorris ; the last thing he said was that the joy was worth all the pain."

Dorris clung to her. " Did *I* kill him?" she whispered. " Did I break his heart? You said once that I would!"

Her sister did not answer.

" Oh! I wish I had been better to him! I never believed he was going to die ! Oh, Sissy! the thought of him will haunt me forever and ever and ever! Did I break his heart? Say no! no! no!"

She was working herself into a frenzy, and her eyes demanded an answer.

" I think God wanted to give him a

greater joy than ever your love could be-
stow, Dorris, so He took him to Himself.
He needs nothing now ; his bliss is com-
plete."

Her words fell on deaf ears. Dorris
was sobbing out all her remorse and terror in her arms.

" Come," she whispered, " let us leave
him to rest in his perfect peace. We
must go on living."

The world was not surprised to hear of
John Dryden's death, and many there
were to blame the frivolous young wife,
but some sighed pityingly as they
watched the slight figure, in its heavy
crepe, going about with half-frightened,
haunted eyes.

The will was opened, and, with the
exception of a legacy to Leigh Kurt and
his wife, all John Dryden's wealth was
left to his wife *as long as she remained
his widow!* In case of her remarriage
the entire fortune passed to a distant
relative.

At first, Dorris would not believe in the

irrevocableness of this decree of the dead man's jealousy, but, when convinced, she went about like one stunned, with a strange despair in her eyes.

Slowly the sultry summer days wore away, and gradually the apathy which had enveloped her gave place to a feverish restlessness.

The sound of the door-bell caused her to start nervously. She trembled perceptibly when she opened the mail bag, and, at last, that which she waited for, came.

CHAPTER XV.

Allan Kip entered the room where Dorris and her sister sat, unannounced.

He was looking eager, young, full of hope and happiness, but Dorris would not meet his eyes.

Mrs. Kurt rose to leave the room soon after he came in, but resumed her seat when she caught an imploring glance from her sister.

She did her best to give some life to the conversation, but Dorris sat silent and Allan gave her random replies as he let his gaze devour the small, black-robed figure, with eyes full of leaping love-light. She found her task impossible, and rose at last with a decision which paid no heed to imploring glances.

As she left the room, the sound of an impulsive movement and smothered cry of joy reached her ear.

"Thank God!" she ejaculated. " Love will make a woman of her, and she will know true happiness at last!"

And Dorris?

Her face was hidden on Allan's breast.

" Don't cry, sweetheart!" he whispered. "All our troubles are over; a life of love lies before us! Think of it, my beautiful, we will be forever together, together, together. Ah! what a heaven that will be! Do you know how I have yearned for a glimpse of your face, the sound of your voice, a touch of this soft, little hand?"

He kissed the fingers.

" But all the mysery is past! Now I shall have you always near me, giving me inspiration by your beauty, comfort in your love, and joy through your joyousness !"

" Look up at me, my sweet. I came to you the moment the news of your freedom reached me in the desert where I and my grief were hiding. Look up and tell me you are glad, let me hear you

say you love me. Why, Dorris, what
makes you look so strangely?"

The face she raised to his was white,
the lids drooped over eyes that were filled
with a sort of dumb terror. He gazed at
her, and his close clasp loosened; dread
quenched his joy.

"What is it?" he cried.

She struggled to reply, but her trembling lips refused to do her bidding.

"Dorris, you torture me. Speak?"

"I can't; I am afraid!" she whispered.

"Afraid? Are you hiding some secret
from me that will prevent our marriage?"

She shivered. "Yes, the will!"

For a moment he looked at her in un-
comprehending perplexity, then a sudden
storm broke over him.

"The will!" he cried, flinging her
from him. "The will, which robs you
of your wealth at your remarriage! Is it
that which has come between us! You
would give up such love as I give you for
a life of empty luxury? You would
blight my soul to robe your body in laces

and satins? You would sell your God-given womanhood for a mess of pottage?"

He stopped, choked by his passion.

Cowering, she stood before him, hiding her face in her hands.

"'And you told me that you loved me!" he cried, his words tumbling over one another like leaping flames. "Love!" Such women as you desecrate the word. What can soulless beings know of its divine meaning? Oh! you beautiful, worthless bauble of flesh and blood. What fiend gives you your power to win the adoration of true-hearted men?"

His voice broke in a sob, and at the sound she raised her face to his, tear-wet, pleading; so like a tender, innocent child's, asking for pardon.

"I do love you!" she faltered. "But you can't understand how afraid I am to be poor! If I married you and had to live as I did in the old days, I might grow to be sorry. I can't help it. I think this dread of poverty was born in me. I can't overcome the fear of it! Just wait,

that's all I ask. Wait 'till you can become a great artist, so we won't have to
be very poor, and then——"

He cut her short with a gesture of
command, and turned away towards the
door. " God help me!" she heard him
murmur.

Was he going to leave her? " Allan!"
she cried, grasping a chair to keep herself from falling. "Allan! Allan! Oh,
come back—listen to me. I can't have
you go away! I love you—oh, I do love
you——"

The door shut sharply upon her cry,
leaving her alone in her shame and
despair.

Mrs. Kurt, hearing the front door close
behind him, ran down stairs with joyous
congratulations upon her lips, but stopped
in amazement as her eyes fell upon her
sister, standing white and rigid in the
middle of the room.

" What has happened?" she cried.

" Allan hates me—he flung me away

from him. Oh! I cannot tell you how terrible he .was!"

Mrs. Kurt's face flushed. "How dared he?" she exclaimed.

Dorris threw herself upon the couch, burying her head in the pillows. "I told him I was *afraid* to be *poor!*" she sobbed, "and he wouldn't listen while I explained it to him. He called me dreadful things, and left me, and oh, Sissy, I didn't know 'till now, how much I do love him!"

"How could a woman with a soul treat the man she loved like that?" cried her sister.

"Oh don't! don't! That's what he said. You ought to understand, Sissy. You've often told me that you believed I was impressed with the horror of poverty before I was born. Mother and father and you were so awfully poor then. I can't help it. I tell you I dread it as I do death!"

The scorn in her sister's eyes softened. "That is true," she said, thoughtfully.

" Perhaps I am judging you harshly, but, oh, Dorris, are you only a butterfly that dances brightly when the sun shines and hides in terror when the clouds draw near?"

Choking sobs were her only answer. She sighed and stroked the tumbled hair.

" There, don't work yourself into a fit of sickness with your crying. God made the butterflies as well as the greater things of life, so he must have some use for them, and if you can only exist in the sunshine you'll have to have it, I suppose, so don't fret. Allan will come back to you."

Her words comforted Dorris, and gradually her sobbing ceased.

But the days came and went, and brought no sign from Allan.

CHAPTER XVI.

Christmas bells made merry music through the frosty air.

Mrs. Kurt sat in a low chair beside the fire, cradling in her arms a fleecy bundle of laces and flannels.

Dorris lay at full length in an easy chair near-by, and Leigh stood at the window, turning now and then to feast his happy eyes on the picture before the fire.

"Every one seems to be in such a jolly mood," he said. "I have been counting the faces that passed, and nine out of ten have been wreathed in smiles. Is it so every Christmas? I've never noticed it before."

His wife smiled, resting her cheek against the downy head nestling in her arms. "It is your own joy you see reflected," she said. "I think I never knew the real meaning of love until now; it is the embodied spirit of Christmas in my soul!"

Dorris rose abruptly. " I'm going out," she exclaimed. " The atmosphere of this nursery is stifling."

" What makes her so low in her spirits to-day," asked Leigh, when the door had closed behind her. " Has she seen the announcement in the paper?"

" I haven't seen it myself—tell me about it."

" Why, Allan Kip has inherited a fortune from his uncle in England—a gay old batchelor, who has just died. No one knew he stood in for such luck. He posed as a poor genius, you know. He intends to leave this country for good, now."

The young mother's face clouded. " If that is so, Dorris will never win him back, I fear! I so hoped he would forgive her. She really loves him, poor child!"

"She was a little fool to act as she did,"

he replied, with masculine lack of sympathy, and then the baby awoke and all other interests were forgotten in coaxing her ladyship to smile.

Two days later Dorris brought a letter to her sister.

"Read it," she said, turning away her face.

"But I—I would rather not," answered the other, seeing it was addressed to Allan Kip.

"You must! I can't keep silence any longer. I shall die if he goes away forever, as they say he is going to do! Oh, Sissy! I know now what love is! At last I have found my soul! Read my letter, and tell me if I have written what will most surely let him see all that is in my heart for him. I don't know what I have said, my brain is on fire, help me!"

She turned away and her sister opened the letter. Her lashes were heavy with tears as she read its contents and returned it to Dorris.

"If he were a woman, he would come

back to you, my darling," she said, answering the question in the eyes raised to her's. "But forgiveness is not part of a man's love. They do not understand as we do."

The day seemed endless after the letter was sent. Luncheon was a silent meal, and Dorris spent the afternoon in listening for the door-bell. She wandered into the nursery as the twilight fell and sat watching her sister, rocking to and fro, singing a low lullaby to the child in her arms.

"I wish I was your baby, Sissy," she murmured. "I feel so tired and I think it would rest me to have you rock and sing to me like that."

Mrs. Kurt was about to answer, when the door opened and a maid brought a note to Dorris. The small fingers trembled so that they could scarcely open the envelope, but the few words were read in one swift glance.

"My newly acquired fortune does not remove the obstacle to our marriage.

Love, void of respect, must prove unsat-
isfying. I leave for England to-night."

Slowly the paper fluttered to the
ground.

"Oh, Dorris, darling! What has he
said?"

Laying the sleeping baby in its crib, she
ran to her sister's side, but the white face
smiled at her in a way that checked her
words.

"Read it!" answered a voice that
sounded like the wind from ice-bound
seas.

She picked up the fallen sheet and
read the brief note, then flung her arms
about the rigid form.

"Oh, my poor little sister, it is as I
said, men can not forgive!"

Young Mrs. Dryden drew herself
away from the clinging embrace.

"No!" the new note in her voice
startled her sister, and she laughed in a
way that brought tears into Mrs. Kurt's
eyes.

"As a new sensation, though, this is

positively invaluable—it's a climax!" she
continued as she moved across the room,
her head held very high and a haughty
smile curving her lips. "I am like the
man in Grimm's fairy tale, who wanted
to learn to 'shiver.' At last I have
learned what a real sensation is like. My
wish has been granted and I am quite
satisfied! Aren't you glad, Sissy? I am!
So glad that ——"

The proud head drooped suddenly and
Mrs. Kurt sprang forward just in time to
save her sister from falling heavily to the
floor.

CHAPTER XVII.

Time is a master artist.

Dipping his fateful finger into the well of experience, he traces upon human hearts, strange images, unguessed possibilities.

Five years had changed young Mrs. Dryden and to-night, as she sat playing dreamy lullabies to the drowsy child on her sister's knee, she made a sweet picture of womanhood, full of that subtle tenderness which crowns all true women with a halo of sacred beauty.

"This paper has devoted one entire column to praises of you and your many charities, Dorris."

Leigh glanced up at her and smiled. "They can't say enough of your generosity!"

She turned from the piano and joined

the group about the table, pausing beside
her sister's chair to stroke the child's
curls.

" Don't you think that happiness sometimes makes people selfish?" she asked.
" In the old days, I never used to think
about any one but myself, but now I
want to relieve all the suffering I see. I
can't bear to think there is any one else
in the world who is as heavy hearted as I
am!"

Leigh rattled the paper briskly—men
are fearful of tears in a woman's voice—
but Louise looked up into her sister's face
with a fond smile.

"Every cloud has its silver lining, darling, and so will yours, some day."

Dorris shook her head. "He will never
come back to me. Never! "

A smothered exclamation from Leigh
drew their attention.

"What is it?" asked his wife.

"Nothing, nothing!" he answered,
turning the paper hastily, but not before
Dorris had caught sight of the glaring

headlines "Lost! A Fortune! Strange history of the well-known artist, Allan Kip!"

Her face grew white. "Oh, read it, quick!" she cried.

Leigh turned back to the page with muttered misgivings.

" ' Truth is stranger than fiction,' as we all know," the article began, " and this old saying is once more proven correct by the events which have transpired in the life of one of our leading artists, Mr. Allan Kip.

" Being a true lover of his art, he disdained the aid of his uncle's money, and worked his way to fame on the merits of his genius alone.

" Even his intimate friends supposed him to be penniless, with no expectations of a material nature, until, through his uncle's death, he fell heir to vast wealth, five years ago.

"He made good use of his great fortune in many ways and he now stands an acknowledged artist of the greatest genius, his fame undisputed by even the most severe critics. Suddenly, however, in the midst of his prosperity comes a most unforeseen calamity of rather a sensational nature."

Leigh paused, glancing nervously at Dorris, who leaned against his chair, with eyes full of dread.

"Go on; I can bear it!" she whispered.

"It seems that the uncle whose fortune Mr. Kip inherited, had led a roving life, spending his youth in reckless dissipation. Under the influence of drink, he had married a woman of equally disreputable habits; deserting her as soon as reason returned to him and never seeing her afterwards. Now, however, the son of that mad union appears to claim the property, as its legitimate heir, bearing with him papers that prove the dead man to be his lawful father.

"As Mr. Kip fell heir to the estate simply through being the next in succession and not by will, this robs him of wealth, and casts him upon the world with only his fame as his fortune once more.

"We regret his loss, but learn we are to be congratulated as a people, inasmuch as he has been forced to accept the work of painting the pictures for the new Cathedral, and will therefore make his home in this city for some time to come."

No one spoke as Leigh stopped reading. He pretended to be absorbed in the stock report, and Louise kept her head bent low over her child's sleeping form.

Dorris stole to her side, pressing a tear-wet face against her cheek. "Sissy," she whispered, tremulously, "If he comes home, I am going to him."

CHAPTER XVIII.

An air of artistic harmony hung about the studio.

Rugs, draperies, statuary, paintings—all formed a whole that rested the eye and soothed the senses.

At an easel in the center of the room, sat a tall, broad-shouldered man. His brown velvet coat showed dabs of paint here and there, and a long pipe occasionally sent forth blue clouds of smoke, which hung about his handsome head like some mystic halo. An irritable frown creased his forehead and he tossed his brushes aside with an impatient sigh.

" I can't keep my thoughts upon my work !" he muttered. " The very air of this place is filled with the memory of her. These sea breezes seem to bear to me the perfume of her hair; the chimes of the old Cathedral sound like the music of her laugh. Fool! Shall I never be able to forget her empty loveliness?"

He threw himself wearily upon the couch, surrendering his thoughts to the haunting memories, until his eyes grew tender, and his lips softened into a dreamy smile,

A knock sounded, but he did not hear it, and then the door was pushed timidly open, and a slender woman's figure stood hesitatingly on the threshold.

Her eyes drew his gaze by the intensity of their regard.

With a smothered cry he sprang to his feet. " *You!*" he whispered, breathlessly.

He went towards her slowly, as if doubting the evidence of his senses, and she stood waiting for him with piteous face raised pleadingly.

He came close; he touched her arm, and then the softened love-look fled from his eyes.

" What is it you want here?" he

asked, harshly. " Have you come to patronize the poor artist ?"

She clasped her hands nervously and her lips trembled as she opened them to speak.

" I have come to—to—oh, Allan! I couldn't stay away. I longed so to see you again !"

A hot flush surged over his face; he moved nearer her impulsively. "Dorris!" he whispered. " Dorris! Dorris! Do you love me?"

She put out both hands to him. " Oh, yes! yes!" she sobbed. " Take me back into your heart again, Allan—take me back !"

He caught her in his arms with an in-articulate cry of joy, and the weary past was blotted out forever.

An hour later, as they drove home-ward in her carriage, he turned to her with sudden misgivings in his eyes.

" But, Dorris!" he exclaimed, "have you forgotten? I have lost my fortune now. I am only a poor artist, who earns his daily bread by the labor of his brain. We will be poor, child. Oh, have you forgotten that?"

"Don't!" she whispered, creeping closer to his side, with down-cast eyes and tear-wet lashes. "Don't remind me of what I used to be—it is too dreadful. Love has given me a soul, and pain has taught me joy!"

THE SENATOR'S WOOING.

IT was long past midnight, and the ball was drawing to an end. Society's buds were looking wilted, and chaperones began to nod like full blown roses, whose petals might drop and scatter at a touch of time. It had been a cosmopolitan affair, as everything must be in Washington, but decidedly chic. Foreign Ambassadors adorned the rooms like bric-a-brac, while many a literary and artistic lion shed the light of genius upon less gifted fellows. The hostess drew a sigh of mingled weariness and content as her eyes dwelt upon the scene before her. It had been a success, she told herself, and an expression of satisfaction rested upon her face.

"Must you go so soon?" she asked, as Senator Calvin and Miss Thurston ap-

proached her—for it had been not the
least of her triumph to receive these two
leaders of the social and Senatorial cir-
cles, and as she bade them adieu, she voiced
to herself again the question which society had asked itself many times. But
that which society asks itself, often gets
for its answer only a larger question
back. Meantime the principal actors
enjoyed themselves quite unconscious of
the perplexities they occasioned.

"Are you cold?" asked the Senator, as
he drew the cloak about his companion,
and noticed her shiver slightly.

"Yes," she answered, with a laugh,
"I am not accustomed to 'lobbying,' you
know. I wish my carriage would come."

"It will be called in a moment; come
back into the hall and wait," said the
Senator, adding in a tone approaching
solicitude, "I hope you have not taken
cold."

The evident tenderness of the Senator's
manner brought a flush to Miss Thurston's cheek, and she raised her eyes to his

with an expression which confused him,
for he was not used to the ways of
women ; he considered them incompre-
hensible. There was a slight pause while
he drew her into a sheltered nook, and
then he said in his usual tone :

" I am coming to see you soon, to dis-
cuss the new bill before the Senate.   I
want   your   judgment on,—what's the
matter?" he interrupted himself, as he
noticed the quizzical expression on his
companion's face.   She   shrugged her
shoulders, half laughing.   " How long
have I been giving you the result of my
woman's instinct, and helping you out
of those stupid political tangles, in direct
opposition to your constitution, which
forbids women to meddle ?"

The Senator's face brightened with a
sudden smile as he answered, " I could
never pay you all I owe"——

" What, going?" exclaimed a bright
voice, and, with a start, they turned to
see a gay little woman tripping across
the hallway toward them. " Sensible.

girl! I wish I could do likewise," she runs on. " But Edward has been glued to the whist table since 10 o'clock, and I suppose he will stick there until the others are sent for by their wives, when he will wake to the realization of his duty to me !"

Mary Thurston laughed amusedly.

" You are always such a martyr, Jean, my dear," she said, adding over her shoulder, as she was led away, " shall I see you at the woman's meeting to-morrow morning?"

The little woman shrugged her shoulders. " If I get away from here by that time, yes," she answered, and stood watching them as they disappeared in the darkness beyond.

" I wonder if he did it to-night," she said to herself. " If he didn't—well, he just doesn't deserve to get her, that's all !"

" May I have this dance?" asked a voice at her side.

" Thank you, but I am engaged to Senator Calvin," she answered, as she saw that genlteman's tall form advancing, with snow powdered hair. " You came just in time to save me," she exclaimed, as he drew her arm through his. " That odious little Cottrel asked me for this number, and I told him it was yours."

" Then we will have to take a turn or two for his benefit, I suppose," answered the Senator, and they joined the rythm of the moving forms.

" Tell me," the vivacious voice broke forth again, " did you do it to-night?"

The Senator smiled covertly. " Do what? " he asked, in a non-committal tone.

" You know very well!" answered Mrs. Bellaire impatiently, " and just let me tell you, Mr. Senator, if you don't ask Mary Thurston to be your wife pretty soon, some luckier man will get her. She won't wait forever for you."

No response being made to this outburst, the little lady stopped abruptly, disengaging herself from his arm.

"Don't you want to marry her?" she demanded.

"I suppose I do," he replied, with a serious deliberateness. "I should be deeply chagrined if I did not, but there is plenty of time."

"O!" ejaculated Mrs. Bellaire, "if that isn't just like a man! Here you have been showering devotion on Mary for over two seasons, making every one wonder and talk, and yet never giving her a chance to say yes or no. Now you know I love you both better than any one else in the world—excepting Edward, perhaps," she interpolated with a comical little grimace, "and the dearest wish of my heart is to see you two married, but I am losing all patience with you, and I have half a mind to encourage Mary's liking for that charming German, who is so deadly in love with her."

Senator Calvin looked gravely startled. "Von Blon!" he exclaimed. "Does she really fancy him?"

Mrs. Bellaire's eyes brightened with

a sudden smile, which she hid behind drooped lashes. " Fancy him? Hardly ! It is more serious than that ; he is so entirely charming, and makes such an ideal lover," and there is a telling pause, while the music floats about them and mingles with the soft splash of a fountain in the conservatory beyond.

Mrs. Bellaire stole a quick look into the face above her, and a dimple appeared as she said suggestively, " He hasn't proposed to her yet, but he is only waiting his opportunity, and when that comes I pity your chances!"

Senator Calvin looked decidedly perturbed and was about to answer when a cheery voice at their side exclaimed, " Well, well, my dear, I have been looking for you everywhere ; aren't you ready to go home yet?"

Mrs. Bellaire laughed. " Edward," she said, " you ought to have been a woman, you have such a trick of always pretending to be in the right. Now what

was it made you remember me at the
eleventh hour?"

" Stebbins' wife sent for him," con-
fessed the Major, and wondered why his
wife laughed as she/disappeared for her
wraps.

" I think I will go, too," Senator
Calvin said, as they waited together
until Mrs. Bellaire returned, cloaked and
hooded. As she bade him good night she
whispered impressively, " Remember,
there is no time to lose, for once you
must forget the statesman in the lover !"

" My dear," remarked the Major, as
they rolled off into the night, " when
will you stop match-making?   It is dangerous business."

" Nonsense !" answered his wife, blithe-
ly, " Tom Calvin is as deeply in love with
Mary as she is with him, but he is such a
dear old stupid and so absorbed in silly
politics that he has just neglected to propose.   He thinks women and love will
wait !   I am his good angel, and if it were
not for me he would let it go until ho

really did lose the dearest girl in the world."

Her husband laughed, then yawned. " Ah, well, there is nothing so satisfying as duplicate whist," he observed, drowsily, and settled himself for a nap in his corner.

CHAPTER II.

Meanwhile, the Senator walked back to his rooms with a very thoughtful expression. He had loved Mary Thurston for months, and yet, so absorbed had he been, that time had slipped past without his finding space to win her in. She seemed to belong to him by right of their perfect sympathy, and when he met her, he spent the time in relieving his overburdened mind, trusting to her clear judgment and unerring womanly instinct to lead him out of many a political tangle. To lose all this would be an imcomparable grief to him. He must make her his before that German meddler won her from him. But how? To-morrow was full of important meetings; this was a critical time with little chance for freedom. Besides, he remembered Mary

was to be engaged at the woman's meeting. There was nothing for it then but
to send her a note, and, drawing to him
pen and paper, he began to write. How
weakly sentimental the words looked on
paper! The Senator tossed the sheet into
the fire, and in his solitude he blushed.
After all what were a few days? She
was not likely, he assured himself, to see
Von Blon in that short time, and as soon
as the most important bill, which was
engaging the entire attention of one of
his committees, had passed, he would go
in a sensible way and ask her to be his
wife. Having thus disposed of the question he settled back upon the universal
solace of perturbed mankind, and as he
blew soft clouds of smoke into the air, he
sought with all earnestness to frame the
argument upon which the success of the
Revenue bill would so much depend. He
thought much of statistics and some of
logic, and—saw many visions of a beautiful face and a most inconsequential German.

The following days were filled with
excitement in the Senate.   The crisis of
the fight on the Revenue bill approached,
and those newer complications which
have come into modern politics rendered
that which was once a perfunctory contest, on purely party lines, an exciting
fight in which every inch of winning
ground was opened to the strategy of
both sides.

Senator Calvin, in the midst of the
great fight, became utterly absorbed in
the fascinating struggle, and love, becoming frightened, shrank out of sight.

A week went by and what tricks Cupid
might have played it is hard to tell, but
Cupid is not so black as he is often
painted. And one day when matters in the
Senate were nearing a climax, and everything going against the Senator's party,
Cupid played a trump card. Senator Calvin, being unable to endure the strain in
quiet, at last left the Chamber to walk
off a little of his suppressed excitement
in the corridors outside, and there ran

against Mrs. Bellaire and Mary Thurston
on their way to the ladies' gallery.

" Oh Senator!" exclaimed Mrs. Bellaire, darting up to him, "we have come
to hear your speech.   I just couldn't stay
at home, so I made Mary come with me.
Are we not in time? You look so fagged!
What's the matter, anyway?"

He laughed nervously. "It's a clear
case of narrow rationalism," he answered,
with scarcely repressed irritation. "They
simply won't believe what they can't see
right under their very noses!"

Mrs. Bellaire smiled; "That is a fail-
ing of men, especially in politics, I have
observed," and then she settled herself to
listen to what was going on.

As the Senator dropped into a seat beside Miss Thurston, she turned to him
with a look that was in itself a sedative.
"You are nervous," she said.

He drew his hand wearily across his
forehead.   "It has been a hard day."

She bent impulsively toward him for
an instant, and then, biting her lip,

leaned back in her seat, fastening her attention upon the Senator from Georgia, whose ringing voice was so eloquently holding the attention of the Senate upon the side of the question to which Senator Calvin was opposed, and the color came and went upon her cheek, as suppressed waves of excitement told of the keen interest she felt in the outcome of the contest. As the orator drew toward the close of his argument, she turned with ill-concealed anxiety to the man beside her, "Your speech comes next, doesn't it?"

"Yes," he replied wearily, "I wish it were well over. There is so much at stake, and to tell the truth," he said, dropping into a confidential tone, "the odds are much against us."

"Odds are nothing," said Mary, and her glance now was more of a stimulant than a sedative, for the glances of women are but the rays of soul which no spectroscope has ever analyzed, and no prism has ever subjugated. "Odds," she continued, " are but the atmosphere in which ·

real effort best thrives. If you went upon
the floor of the Chamber in serene confidence, you would feel no necessity for
effort. But to-day, feeling the sweep of
the current so strong against you, you
must rise to your highest effort, and you
will win! Remember," she continued
archly, "I am here and I must not see
you, my friend, encompassed by defeat!"

Before he had time to reply, a page
handed him a peremptory note from a
colleague, calling him to the floor of the
Senate to take his place in the ranks.
And so it happened that, as he stepped
into the midst of the fray, it was not
with the load of his eloquent opponent
upon his mind, but rather with that firm
confidence of victory which had been
borne of the encouragement and hope
held out by Mary.

For two hours the Senate was under
the spell of such magnetic oratory as it
had not had during that session, and such
as had never before come from the lips
of Senator Calvin. Limb from limb,

and joint from joint, he tore apart the
structure his opponent had reared, and
step by step he led his hearers up those
stairs of logic, which, if they be well
built, lead to but one conclusion, and to
that one irresistibly. And, as he spoke,
he knew that he was winning, and each
pulse of victory through his veins served
but to add the certainty of directness of
the sledge-hammer blows of his telling
arguments. As he took his seat, his
eyes sought the ladies' gallery and caught
a glance from Mary Thurston which
glowed with delight, while Mrs. Bellaire
waved her handkerchief at him in defiance of decorum. He watched them as
they left, wishing he could join them,
but that being impossible, contented himself by remembering that he would meet
Miss Thurston on the following evening
at the Dartforth musicale.

CHAPTER III.

The next day proved to be one of those capricious winter days that unconsciously affect us. The morning was bright and clear, but at noon a moody gray mist fell upon the city and a slight, drizzling rain set in. Senator Calvin was feeling the effects of the nervous strain he had been under during the past two weeks, and Dame Nature's fickle behavior affected him disagreeably. He called on Miss Thurston, but she was out,—and he wondered why she should go out in such beastly weather. Later he dropped in at Mrs. Bellaire's and had the good fortune to find that little lady toasting her pretty toes before a glowing fire. She was full of congratulations and delight, and overwhelmed him with praises and compliments. At last she exclaimed :

"But I wasn't half as proud of you as was Mary. I never saw her look so pleased over anything before; that is, until Von Blon joined us in the corridor and then, somehow, he spoiled things!"'

The Senator frowned into the fire. "What do you mean?" he asked.

"Well," continued Mrs. Bellaire, puckering her forehead. "he said, 'Yes, Calvin did very well, but he shows his brains only in the Senate. I often wonder where he keeps his wits when in society,' and Mary just bit her lip and turned away, and I don't know whether she did it to conceal a smile, or an angry answer. Of course I told the simpering man that you saved your wits for those who could appreciate them! He just said it in spite, any way, you know."

The Senator rose and walked restlessly about the room. "Von Blon is right," he said at last, rather bitterly. "I was never intended for a carpet knight. I am absent-minded and preoccupied and dull. I wish he had not said it though

before Mary—I mean Miss Thurston.
And she smiled—No? Tried not to smile,
then, it's the same thing. See"—and he
paused in his restless walk up and down.
" I have reached the zenith of power. I
rule men, I sway a nation, and yet I
have not that grace of manner, that
charm of speech which alone pleases a
woman, even the wisest of them. What
a parody is Life, after all! I have
worked for this end for years and, now
it is attained, I seem to care nothing for
it. I would exchange all my honors for
that easy charm Von Blon possesses—for
the power to make Mary Thurston love
me !"

Mrs. Bellaire rose and laid her hand
on his arm, " I think she does care for
you," she said, "but tell me, why are
you so deeply in love all of a sudden ; is
it jealousy?"

"Perhaps," admitted the Senator. " I
always felt sure of her before."

Mrs. Bellaire smiled. " Let no man
be sure of any woman," she said, oracu-

larly, adding seriously : "If you want
Mary Thurston to be your wife, you
must not give Von Blon any more
chances. He is a persistent lover, and
women too often yield to persistency,
even against their better judgment."

Senator Calvin took the small jewelled
fingers in his, "I shall see her to-night,"
he said significantly, with a look of determination in his eyes, and raising the
hand he held to his lips, he left the room
and house.

CHAPTER IV.

Several hours later found him in the midst of a brilliant throng of society's music-loving butterflies. His eyes eagerly sought for the the stately form he knew so well, but it was some time before he caught sight of her in the music room, apparently quite absorbed in something Von Blon was whispering to her under cover of the music. He tried to reach her side, but had to pay the penalty of greatness by having his progress impeded with friends and acquaintances, who insisted upon shaking hands and congratulating him upon his triumph.

Perhaps, Von Blon saw his slow approach, at any rate, when the Senator at last shook himself free from his followers, Miss Thurston was no where to be seen, and half an hour later he had a vision of

Von Blon's fair head bending over her, as he piloted her to her carriage. After this there was nothing more to keep him, so he soon made his adieu, and went home to his lonely rooms. Never before had such a thing as this occurred! Had Mary seen him, and wished to avoid him? Was she beginning to resent his cool assumption of right to her, or did she really care for Von Blon?

These and similar pleasant thoughts, kept him tossing sleeplessly until morning dawned, when he rose unrefreshed. The day was equally uncomfortable. He could settle to nothing. One moment he decided to write her, and the next fell into despair at the thought of all a refusal would mean to him.

"What a farce a man is, with all his vaunted power!" he said to himself. What power on earth can compare to that a woman wields? If we rule the world, they rule us! It is a delicious misery—this Love!" At last the twilight fell and warned him it was time to dress

for a dinner engagement at Senator
Maxwell's. He was almost glad of the
chance to escape his own thoughts, and,
ten minutes before the dinner hour, entered the Maxwell drawing-room.

Some one in a soft gray gown stood
talking to the hostess, and, as he approached, his beating heart told him it
was Mary. She gave him her hand with
her usual charming frankness and allowed
him to hold it a trifle longer than his
wont, as she told him how glad she was
over his victory in the Senate.

" It was you who won it," he answered,
bending to look into her eyes, and adding
in a low voice, " it was the inspiration of
your words which carried me through,
and I can only hope——"

" Pardon, my dear Senator, but Mrs.
Maxwell has asked me to take Miss
Thurston out to dinner," said a voice
at his side, and Von Blon smilingly offered
his arm to Miss Thurston.

For a moment the Senator looked un-
deniably savage, but quickly recovering

himself, bowed and stepped back, while
Mrs. Maxwell assigned him to an elderly
dowager, and they followed the others
out to the flower-decked table. Mrs.
Bellaire was his vis-a-vis, but Mary and
the German were at the other end of the
long table. Could Fate be more adverse?
What could give Von Blon a better opportunity than the long tete-a-tete of a
course dinner? Of course he would propose.

Senator Calvin groaned inwardly.
Why had he played this fool's part of
procrastination? What fiend of com-
plaisance had possessed him all these
months? His eyes met those of Mrs.
Bellaire across the table, and she drew a
long face—glancing significantly down
to where Von Blon bent over his companion. The German was not touching his food, but kept his eyes fastened on his companion's half averted
face, while she listened to his words with
a sweet seriousness, which sent the blood

back to the Senator's heart with a rush
of despair.

The laughter and chat grew dim in
his ears, and a great bitterness entered
his soul. Of what use was his brilliant
future if Mary did not share it with him?
He was overcome with a sick loathing
for this ambition which had robbed him
of a sweet and noble wife. Again his
glance fell upon the face of the woman
he loved, and as he gazes, a sudden blush
tinges her cheek. The sight maddens
the Senator! Is he to lose her before his
very eyes?

"Now or never!" he muttered to himself in desperation, and taking a visiting
card from his pocket wrote feverishly,
"Will you be my wife?" signing his
initials.

Beckoning to a waiter, he thrust the
folded missive into his hand. "Do you
see that lady in grey, with the diamond
star in her hair?" he asked.

The man's glance followed his and

rested upon the unconscious Miss Thurston. " Yes, sir," he replied.

" I want you to give her this note and
bring me back her answer," the Senator
said, and the man nodded comprehend-
ingly as he started on his errand.

Anxiously the Senator's eyes followed
him till he stood behind Mary's chair,
and quietly slipped the note into her
lap. She looked surprised, but opened
it at once and read the words at a glance.
Without a moment's hesitation she turned
her head and threw the answer over her
shoulder to the waiting messenger, who
turned to bring back the reply.

Not a glance in his direction ! Not a
moment's hesitance in her answer ! What
could that mean but that she scorned his
long delay and this sudden abruptness?
He had lost her then, while Von Blon had
won the sweetest woman in the world.
And it was all his own fault—no woman
likes such things to be taken too much
for granted, yet she must have known he
loved her, though he had not said so in

plain words ! Well ! she was revenged upon him now—ah, would she ever know what a blow it was to lose her? A black cloud of despair engulfed the future, but the waiter's hand upon his shoulder roused him.

" The lady said, ' tell the gentleman I say yes,' " murmured the man's voice in his ear, and Mrs. Bellaire's laugh floated to him from across the table.

Keeping Up Appearances.

"YOU can't go, Helen, you haven't a decent gown to your name!"

"But I must, mother! Nell would never forgive me if I failed her this time, and what could I do if she cast me off? I should be a nobody if she wasn't my friend. You know that!"

"Well, worse things could happen to you, I'm sure! Her friendship brings you small pleasure and only results in your being a slave to her caprice. I'm tired of it all. I wish you were content to live in your own station of life, and not tag on to the skirts of the rich!"

The fretful voice ceased as a heavy step sounded outside.

"What's the matter now?" exclaimed the newcomer, frowning upon them from the doorway.

"Mother says I can't go to Nell's!"

"Well, what of that! Weren't you abroad with her all winter? Can't you stay at home and help your mother for a month or two without whining, I'd like to know? I want this noise to stop, now! I can't write when you two women are wailing up here like tom cats!"

He turned upon his heel and went down stairs again, closing his study door behind him, and silence once more reigned.

"There!" said her mother, "I told you how it would be."

Helen threw herself upon the bed. "Oh! I hate him, and this ugly, sordid life!" she cried, bursting into tears.

"You're an ungrateful child, that's what you are," cried her mother, closing the door with a noisy click as she left the room.

Helen sobbed on until she was exhausted, and then lay staring at the dingy wall paper. The cheap little clock annoyed her by its noisy ticking. How different it was from the dainty French affairs that pointed out the time in Nell's beautiful home. Helen raised herself, and gazed about the small room she called her own. Very bare and homely it looked, in spite of her efforts to make it elegant by a chintz imitation of Nell's luxurious boudoir. She caught a reflection of her face in the opposite glass. "Heavens!" how old I look!" she cried, and the tears flowed afresh.

What was the use of it all, anyway? Her mother was right; Nell's friendship gave her no pleasure, and this constant effort to keep up with the gay people in her set was a severe strain, with no really satisfying results; and yet, could she give it all up—the whirl of pleasures, the excitement, the eclat for the vulgar economy of a dreary life in this so-called home? No! no! a thousand times no!

She laughed mirthlessly, and, rousing herself, set about packing her trunk.

"I'll have Nell's maid to fix up this old Swiss muslin with some cast-off laces," she murmured to herself, "and there is that ball gown she promised me, I think I can tinker that up all right, though I suppose everyone will see it is a cast-off dud! They know I am only a sort of Cinderella, anyway," and she smiled bitterly to herself, as she moved about the room.

"This hat will never stand another season; I must fix up a toque of some kind to help out," she sighed, turning out the contents of a box of scraps, and putting together stray bits of finery with deft fingers that soon transformed the odd pieces of ribbon, lace and velvet into a charming Parisian affair, whose jaunty dash almost restored her to good humor. "Practice makes perfect," she muttered, "I wonder if it is my fate to be forever shabby genteel!"

The tea bell put an end to her preparations, but she went down stairs with her head full of plans for furbishing up her scanty wardrobe through the help of Nell's French maid.

The twins were unusually irrepressible that night and their boisterous behavior kept her father constantly scolding, while her mother fretted in her continuous, nagging way. Two-year-old Betty persisted in hammering her waiter with a spoon, and Helen's nerves were further rasped by the slip-shod appearance of the maid.

" You needn't sit there with your nose stuck in the air if you have been to Europe with Nell Carlton!" cried one of the twins, thereby drawing her father's attention to her.

"Have you been helping your mother this afternoon?" he asked.

"No. I have been getting ready to go to Nell's to-morrow."

He struck the table with his fist. " I told you you were to stay at home and help your mother!" he cried. " I'll not have you gallivanting round like a lazy good-for-nothing. Do you hear?"

" Yes, I hear," answered the girl.

"And I intend you shall obey!" he cried, angrily.

She shrugged her shoulders and rose to leave the table.

"Where are you going?" he called after her.

"To finish my packing!" she answered, defiantly, shutting the door behind her with a bang.

He sprang from his seat, as if to follow her, but apparently changed his mind. "Nice daughter, she is!" he sneered. "Let her go, I say; she's too devilish disagreeable to want around, any way!"

And up-stairs, Helen worked far into the night, over her preparations for departure.

CHAPTER II.

" Hello, Helen, that you?"

The lazy voice proceeded from a nest of luxurious pillows, where a white-robed figure nestled. A maid knelt beside the couch, diligently polishing the nails on each taper finger.

"I hardly expected so prompt a reply to my telegram," the sleepy voice continued ; " but I'm glad you came at once. Dick Dudley is here and I want to keep him all to myself, you know, so you are to make yourself useful by doing the agreeable to a friend of papa's who is staying with us."

A quick flush mounted to Helen's cheek. "Of course, I knew you had something for me to do, or you wouldn't have asked me down !" she said.

" Of course," assented the other. " Adele, don't file that nail so close."

Helen walked restlessly about the room. " He, the one you are to relieve me of, is really very jolly. If it weren't for Dick, I might like him myself; but, of course, I care more for Dick than I could for any one else, and it was most inconsiderate of papa to ask Mr. Nettleton down, when he knows Dick's regiment is ordered out in a month. However, I thought of you, luckily, and now you can take him off my hands."

Helen bit her lips. "I'll go to my room now," was all she said as she turned away."

What right had Nell to treat her in this way? Had they not been playfellows in the old days, before Nell's father had made his money? How they had loved each other then, too! The hot tears filled her eyes, blinding her so that she did not see the man who stepped aside to let her pass him on the stairs.

He turned and gazed after her. "Poor little girl—heart-broken, it seems ; wonder what makes her cry?" he muttered to himself, as he went upon his way.

An hour later he led a self-possessed, conventional girl to dinner, and wondered if this was his "maiden all forlorn." "Women are queer creatures—actresses, every one of them," he said within himself, as he watched the impassive face beside him.

Dinner was a heavy affair. Nell and Dick were utterly oblivious of everything but themselves, while Mr. Carlton appeared worried and absent-minded, talking spasmodically, as if only at intervals conscious of the presence of the others.

After several fruitless efforts at general conversation, Nettleton turned to his companion with a faint smile; "Let's amuse each other," he said, in a low tone.

She laughed. "Don't you think our vis-a-vis sufficiently amusing?"

He glanced at the two opposite and shook his head. "Who is it that says, 'When happiness is looked at through another man's eyes, it becomes pain?'"

"Do you call that happiness?" she asked.

"Don't you?"

"No! If *I* loved a man I should want him to show his love for me by becoming something I could be proud of. It would make me feel like a goose to be gazed at in that fashion."

"Your ideas belong to the good old days of chivalry, when fair women sent their knights forth to do great deeds," he said, smiling down at her. "I fear you would have been as cruel as the heroine in 'The Glove,' whose pride outran her love."

"Oh, but it didn't!" cried Helen. "She threw her glove among the lions to prove the sincerity of all the vows De Lorge had sworn—not to show her power over him."

Nettleton raised his eyebrows. "That is a new version of the poem—is it original?"

"I thought it was until I read Robert Browning's poem, which shows he had

the same conception of the incident. I
was glad he vindicated her character, for
she is a favorite heroine of mine. She
has always been so misunderstood."

" Is that the key to your sympathy?"
he asked.

She nodded.

" Why?"

She rose, as she saw Nell preparing to
leave the men to their cigars. " We can
only sympathize with griefs we understand—each really weeps for himself,"
she replied, following her friend from
the room.

" That's an odd little girl," said Nettleton, turning back to the table.

" Yes ; unhappy disposition," answered
his host, sipping a cordial with a satisfied
air. "Family poor—girl ambitious. Been
too much with Nell, I reckon. Gets the
taste of high living, and doesn't relish
going back to plain fare. Dick, my boy,
try this liqueur—deuced fine, if I do say
so myself!"

Nettleton lighted his cigar. "It was she, then," he said to himself. "Poor little girl—poor little girl!"

CHAPTER III.

" Nell, may I borrow Adele for five minutes?"

" Good gracious!" aren't you dressed yet? What have you been doing all this time, Helen?"

"Trying to make your cast-off gown look as if it had always belonged to me," replied the girl.

" It does very well," said the other, throwing a glance over her shoulder. " Here is some lace Adele can catch into the bodice, but do hurry, for Dick hates to wait, you know."

Adele's quick fingers soon put the finishing touches to the simple toilet, and Helen joined the waiting group below.

" You look like a water lily in that white gown, with the touches of green about you," Nettleton said, with frank admiration in tone and glance.

" By jove, yes ! She does look nice to-night." chimed in Dick. " Haven't you worn that gown before? It looks sort of natural, you know."

Helen flushed. " It is one of Nellie's last year gowns," she answered, raising her head proudly.

" O !" stammered Dick. " Well, but you've fixed it up deuced cleverly. I hardly recognized it, you see !" and he turned to help Nell into the carriage, feeling he had gotten himself out of that blunder in good form.

Leaning far back in her corner among the cushions, Helen gave herself up to bitter thoughts. Dick called to them from the other carriage, and Nettleton shouted an answer, but she sat still, unheeding.

" Won't you talk to me, please. I'm half asleep," he said, at last.

" No ! my tongue is tipped with worm-wood, to-night, and had best keep quiet," she answered.

He was silent a moment, and then leaned towards her, saying quietly, " I think you are wrong !"

" What do you mean ?" she asked.

"You exaggerate your own grievances, and, forgive me, parade them too much. It was not necessary to tell us the gown had belonged to your friend."

She did not answer, and he went on earnestly.

" Don't be offended, but, during my visit here I have seen your unhappiness, and felt for you deeply, and I want to ask you why you stay on in the false position you are placed in here. It doesn't make you happy!"

" There is nothing else to do," she answered drearily.

" Have you no home of your own, then —no family ties?"

" Yes."

" Then, forgive me again, but why don't you go to those who love and need you? Leave this hot-house existence for the butterflies who belong to it !"

"Oh, you don't understand!" she cried. half sobbing.

His voice drew her irresistibly. She stretched out her hands in the darkness, and felt comforted when he took them in his own.

"Tell me about it. I want to help you if I can, poor little girl."

"They don't love me at home, and I don't love them. It's all so mean and sordid and dull!" she broke forth.

He did not answer, but she felt his clasp loosen.

"I knew you couldn't understand," she cried, "but I can't help it. I hate to be poor, and live in that mean way. People grow narrow, and coarse, and selfish when they have to exist like that!"

He bent nearer her. "Are you sure you are not the selfish one?"

"I!" she exclaimed.

"Sunshine will brighten the most dingy home," he went on. "If you tried to bring happiness into the lives of those who should be as dear as they are

near to you, don't you think they would
soon grow to love you? I know you
would find more content in doing that
than turning your back on duty, and
burning your heart out in this flame of
fashion."

"O! if I only had you to help me,
perhaps I could do it, then! No one
ever talked to me like this before. Why
are you so different from all the other
men Nell knows!"

He half smiled in the darkness.

" I am no more one of Miss Eleanor's
circle than you are. We are equally out
of our element here. Her father and
mine are old time friends, however, and
I have strayed here through that connec-
tion."

" Are all the men like you, then, that
are outside her set?"

He laughed at the question. "Heaven
forbid! But have you really no friends
besides those in Miss Eleanor's circle?"

She shook her head, sighing wearily.
" I've always hung on to Nell's skirts.

She has given me all I have and I am her
body servant, in return."

" Poor child!''

The tenderness in his voice thrilled
her, and the clasp of his fingers on hers
brought a sense of joy into her heart
that was as strangely sweet as new. " I
could die for him!" she whispered to
herself, and sank into a dream that held
her until the carriage drew up before the
porte-cochere.

Nell and Dick had arrived before, and
were not easily found in the crowded
rooms. Dick took possession of Nettleton,
and Nell allowed herself to be borne off
in the arms of a tall, ungainly man, who
piloted her in and out among the throng
by sheer muscular force. Helen subsided
into a corner, from whence she gazed at
the swaying figures, feeling lonely and
set apart, in the midst of so much splendor
and prosperity. Gradually her thoughts
wandered from the gay scene before her,
back to the little bare room at home.
Nettleton's earnest words rang again in

her ears. Was she the selfish one? Could she make life at home brighter if she went patiently to work, and broke the chains that bound her to this life of bitter-sweet? "I could do anything if he would help me!" she whispered to herself, and blushed warmly as she saw the object of her thoughts approaching.

"What, not dancing?" he asked, smiling down at her.

"If I told the truth, I should confess that no one has asked me to do so, but, as you might consider that a 'needless parade of my grievances,' I'll pretend it is too warm to exert one's self so violently."

He laughed. "Come, you are cross. You have been left alone too long; a turn or two with me will wake you up."

He clasped her to him with a gentle pressure, and drew her in among the swaying forms. Helen forgot to breathe. The music throbbed upon the air with a passionate sweetness that made her heart ache, and the touch of his arm filled her with a rapture that was pain. Some one, brushing against them, pressed her close to his side for one short instant, and he glanced down into her eyes.

" You are pale," he murmured ; " are you tired?"

She could not answer. His arm seemed to draw her closer for a moment, and then he roused himself.

" Come, we'll have an ice, and then go home. It's late enough to be respectable, I'm sure."

She followed him unresistingly, still under the spell of the music, with her eyes full of dreams.

"Hello, you two, where have you been hiding? I've looked everywhere for you," cried Dick's voice a few moments later, as he ran across them in the refreshment room.

"We have been dancing, and after we have eaten this, we are going home," Nettleton replied.

"Well, you'll have to take us with you ; that blockhead of a coachman went home after he brought us here, so Nell and I will have to crowd in on you two. Hope you don't mind?"

"Why should we? We are the ones who will be de trop answered Nettleton.

It was a silent party that drove home through the dim, cool night. Helen's eyes were closed, while Nell yawned audibly. It seemed a long time before they drew up before their own door.

"I don't think it pays to go to balls in the country," grumbled Nell, "one feels like a frump after driving five miles to get there, and the distance seems twice as long going home!"

Nettleton turned to Helen as she stood in the shadows.

"Good-night," he murmured, taking her hand in his.

"Will you forgive me for my lecture?"

Her fingers tightened about his. "I am going to try to be unselfish," was all she said, but, after she had gone, he remembered that her eyes had been full of tears.

CHAPTER IV.

It was August, and the air was heavy with heat. Helen had dressed early for dinner, and wandered out into the gathering twilight. The birds were calling drowsily to each other, and the breezes kissed the flowers in a warm caress. All the earth was in a slumberous mood, resting softly in the arms of Nature. The sound of hasty footsteps broke the dreamy quiet, and Helen turned to find Nettleton at her side, with a troubled look in his eyes and a telegram in his hand.

" What has happened?" she cried.

"I am called home. Father is ill—they hope not fatally—but I cannot tell——"

She held out both hands to him. "Oh, how sorry I am!" she said, quick tears filling her eyes.

He clasped her hands close in both his

own. "This is a sad farewell," he murmured, "but I hope it may not be forever."

"Forever?" she cried.

"Promise me one thing," he went on hurriedly, bending his face to hers. "Promise that you will give up this unreal life of shadow-chasing, and go home to bring some sunshine into the lives of those you ought to love!"

She did not answer. Her face seemed carved in marble.

"Promise—for my sake!" he whispered.

Her eyes grew deep with a sudden rapture, and her face held the glory of sunset. "For your sake? I would do anything for you!"

For an instant his face caught the glowing light from hers, and then grew white with pain. "Poor child!" he breathed. "My poor little girl!" A moment more he gazed into her eyes, then stooping, pressed his lips to her forehead and was gone.

She stood where he left her, swaying like the breeze-kissed flowers around her, with eyes strangely bright and lips apart, as if she drank in joy that was half pain. A yellow paper rustled at her feet. It was the message he had dropped—evil messenger of Fate, that took from out her life the only joy she had ever known. Lifting the crumpled thing from where it lay, she smoothed it out and read : "Come at once. Your father ill. We hope not fatally. Margaret."

"Margaret!" Was she his sister? No! The message read "Your father!"

A blinding misery swept over the girl as she stood alone in the gathering gloom. "Forever !" Had he not said the word? Forever—forever—oh, eternity of pain !

"Helen! Helen !" came a voice from the house, but she could not move. The sound of wheels, and voices calling out last good-byes, rang on the evening air. He was gone, then, while she stood there in the night, alone—alone forever !

After what seemed long years of misery, she dragged herself back to the house, longing only for the solitude which dumb creatures seek when they receive their death blow.

"Helen, where have you been?"

Nell's voice startled her into consciousness.

"In the garden—I don't feel well—I'm going to my room," she answered laconically.

"But won't you have dinner first?"

"No, I couldn't eat!"

Slowly she ascended the stairs, as though her heart was too heavy to carry. "I am going home to-morrow, Nell," she called back, passing on to her room without waiting for an answer.

The moonbeams stole in at her window, flooding the place with brightness, and Helen set to work at her packing, with only its light to aid her. She worked on with feverish haste until the last garment was folded away in the small trunk and then, when it was all done, she knelt at the window, resting her head on her arms and yielding to the utter weariness that filled both heart and soul.

The August moon drifted overhead in all its stately splendor, as calm, as serene as if its silver rays did not fall upon the miseries of a world!

"Helen must be asleep, her room is so dark," came Nell's voice from below.

"Why does she go home so suddenly?" put in Dick's baritone.

Nell laughed. "Oh, I only asked her down to amuse Hector Nettleton, you know, and now he's gone, I suppose she knows I don't need her any more."

"Nor want her?"

"Silly boy! I never want any one when I have you!"

An eloquent pause followed, broken at last by Dick.

"Nettleton's a deuced fine fellow; pity he couldn't have fallen in love with Helen, for her sake."

"Oh, he's engaged to a Margaret somebody, you know. Family affair; it was

settled when they were almost children,
I think."

"Queer way of doing things," exclaimed Dick. "I'll bet he doesn't care
a rap for her now."

Their words were lost in the distance
as they strolled on into the night,and only
Nell's flute-like laugh floated back to the
girl at the window.

She raised her face to the sky, all wet
with tears. "Oh, God!" she sobbed;
" I pray that he may love her.   I pray
he may find peace!"

THE TOUCH OF NATURE.

CAPRICIOUS April had arrived to lure forth trusting mortals with its warm smiles, only to lose the sunny mood in petulant bursts of rain.

Gentle breezes murmured among the tree tops, as if the rustling garments of spring were heralding her approach. The park was filled with people, eager to taste the first delights of summer.

" Why do you sigh—are you tired?" asked a tall young man, glancing down at his companion.

" Oh no! I was only wondering how it would seem to own a carriage, and lie among the cushions like that woman over there !"

His glance followed hers.

" I wouldn't have you look as tired and

fretful as she does for all the wealth of the world!" he exclaimed.

" Ah, but *I* should be happy," she replied quickly.

He shook his head. " The hot-house atmosphere that rich women live in is as deadly as—well, as any prison from which Nature is shut out. Don't you see how cold her eyes look? They don't smile with her mouth, poor thing!"

A ripple of laughter broke over his words as if in derision. Several well-groomed men surrounded the carriage, and their gay voices reached the girl and her companion as they passed by, and were lost in the ever-changing throng of faces.

Many envious glances were cast on the gay group that laughed and chatted until the sun sank low, and April changed her mood to one of tears.

"Get in; I'll drop you at the club!" said the soft-voiced woman of luxury, as she made room for one of the men at her side.

" You are charity itself, Mrs. Bolton, and I am favored of the gods. This April weather plays the deuce, doesn't it !"·

She laughed idly.

" O, it's amusing. I like variety even in the weather. Life is so deadly dull !"

" To us poor beggars, yes, but it ought not be to you who are young, lovely, rich and blessed with a husband and children that any woman might envy."

" Heavens ! how bourgeois you are, Jack ! No one ever thinks of including a husband or children among their list of blessings, nowadays ! If you had said I was the acknowledged leader of our set, or had the name of being the best-gowned woman in the city, then I should have felt flattered."

He bent toward her and took her hand in his. " You are the most charming woman on earth," he murmured, letting his eyes dwell upon her face with open admiration. " You know I adore you, but you seem as heartless as· you are lovely. You care only to be admired, not loved."

" Don't preach! It's a bore. Why should one love? It's pleasanter to be amused."

" And are you amused?"

She shrugged her shoulders.

" I wonder what you would do if Tom should lose his grip," he said, meditatively.

"Don't suggest such a horror! Drown myself, probably. I couldn't live without my horses and opera box, now."

" Don't drown yourself—come to me," he whispered.

She laughed. " That would be the step beyond suicide—purgatory!" she said.

" Perhaps not. I could at least give you plenty of money."

" Here is the club at last—do get out and make yourself cheerful over cigars and poker. You're horribly tiresome today."

The carriage door snapped upon him,

but was opened again before the footman had regained his box, and a tall, dark man threw himself back among the cushions as the horses started forward once more.

" Good heavens, Tom! what a bear you are! Look how you have crushed my velvet. Do sit up and don't act like a melo-dramatic goose."

The man at her side bent his head on his hands and groaned aloud.

" We are ruined, Sara," he said, hoarsely. " The bank has closed its doors."

The face beside him grew strangely white, and the delicately gloved hands clenched themselves. She gazed at her husband in silent horror until he lifted his haggard face to meet her eyes.

" I couldn't help it!" he half sobbed. " All these weeks and months I have struggled on, but everything went dead wrong, and when the street found out my condition it was all up with me."

The lines of suffering were sharply

drawn, and his brown eyes misty with pain, but the pleading in their depths went unanswered by the wife at his side, who shrank from his touch and turned her face away.

On and on they rolled while the rain beat against the carriage windows, as if the heavens wept in sympathy with the misery of man.

It was dusk when they drew up before their own door, but the lights were burning in the library and he paused as he reached the threshold.

"Come in here," he said. " I must speak to you—I must tell you—oh, Sara! don't look at me like that. Don't you see how I suffer?"

She stood before him, silent and cold, with a deep fire of resentment burning in her eyes.

" You must have seen how anxious I have been of late," he went on, desperately. " Every one but you knew of my trouble. I have been living the life of a lost soul, while you have flirted and danced away the hours. You are a heartless coquette, a vain woman, a——"

She turned to leave the room, but he sprang before her. " Oh, forgive me !" he cried, his voice harsh with pain. " I am mad, Sara. I didn't mean what I said. It is not for me to reproach you when I have brought such misery upon you."

He caught her hands and pressed them to his forehead.

" Won't you forgive me for it all? I have done my best, dear. Oh, can't you go back to the old days before the money came? We were poor enough then, and yet we were happy. Only give me one word of comfort and I will take courage and work for you night and day."

She drew away from him.

" I do not clearly understand what has happened," she said, coldly. " Are we to lose this house, the carriage, servants, everything? Then be so good as to tell me where I am to go. Shall I be turned into the streets?"

He dropped back from her with a look of despair. "No," he answered. "I have been able to secure one thing from the wreck—a farm, that will at least support us until I have a chance to get on my feet once more."

"A farm!" her scornful voice echoed through the room like the laugh of an evil spirit. "I will make a good farmer's wife!" She glanced at her reflection in the opposite mirror. "My ball gowns will be convenient for dairy work, being already sleeveless, and I can literally 'cast my pearls before swine!'"

She smiled bitterly and turned towards the door.

"Sara!" he cried, "don't leave me like this. I tell you I am not to blame. I did my best."

She paused on the threshold.

"I am your wife," she said, "and I must endure this, but I shall never forgive you for what you have done, never!"

CHAPTER II.

April wept itself out, and May was
ushered in to the sound of wedding bells
and the music of laughter and song. All
the world made merry and Spring
laughed back. The great mansion which
had been the center of feast and frolic so
short a time since, stood silent and cold,
facing the butterfly throngs as if sternly
musing upon the fickleness of friendships
which yesterday embraced and kissed on
both cheeks, and to-day, forgets !

Occasionally some one would glance
at the grimly solitary house as they rolled
by behind their well-groomed horses,
and throw a temporary thought of pity
to the woman who had had to surrender
so much. But Sara had been too successful as a leader and too great a favorite in
society, not to excite a fatal envy among

her circle of women "friends," so there
was a subtle undercurrent of satisfaction
at her downfall.

As for the men of her world—men are
but men! Besides, there are so many
charming women ready and willing to
give them pleasure!

So the silent house frowned resentfully
upon the merry folk who had revelled
within its wide-spreading arms, and
now only laughed as they passed it, in
heartless disregard of the chagrin and
broken ambitions, to which it stood as
monumental witness. Its proud grandeur repelled pity—even cold stone resents
that substitute for true compassion—and,
as there was nowhere a heart that could
give forth sympathy, it closed its shuttered
windows fast, and bore its pain in
silence.

But society laughed on, unheeding, and
was very gay. "Times are better," the
men told each other over their club cock-
tails, and women testified to the fact by
magnificent toilets which turned poor

Spring quite green with envy, and by launching forth into a series of entertainments the brilliancy of which eclipsed all former records.

Every one laughed, every one prospered, every one—forgot! Now and then a man might be heard to mutter that "it was a deuced pity poor old Tom got knocked out just when the tide turned," but when letters came from "poor old Tom," asking for a lift, or a loan, to put him on his feet again, it was not of the return of prosperity upon which he dwelt in his letter of reply.

And so Time passed by, sadly wondering at the manners of men, and Nature laid her magic hand upon the fruit and flowers, the meadows and the grain, and many wondrous things grew and opened under her touch, and slowly ripened to perfection.

Sara felt dimly that she was become a part of all this silent, subtle growth and change. At first the quiet of the country had stifled her; the monotony of her life

strangled her, and at times she had felt
as if on the verge of madness. For
weeks she had shut herself away from
her children, and avoided even a glance
at Tom, whose white, deadened face, irritated and angered her. She resented
his looking like that when it was upon
her the keenest misery fell—upon her, to
whom the surrender of that brilliant existence meant a bitter anguish too great
for words. She felt that she hated him,
in those first weeks of exile, and turned
back into herself until that inner self re-
belled, and cried out for food less bitter.

At last the heat of the long summer
days, together with the fierce and unceas-
ing battle which she fought within herself, brought on an illness, and Tom had
nursed her day and night with a patient,
silent devotion, which, in spite of her
anger and resentment, touched the hidden spring of life in her heart, and
sweetened the bitterness that had poi-
soned her whole soul.

Slowly, as she recovered strength, a

wonderful new life grew silently, and
with subtle stealth in her heart of hearts.
She watched the flowers bud and blos-
som ; the fruit as it ripened under God's
sunlight, and, as the marvelous secrets
of Nature revealed themselves, her soul
grew and taught her the divine mysteries of Life and Love, of Death and
Eternity.

Then it was that her children drew
close to her, with that strange instinct
which leads a child through the intrica-
cies of hearts and souls, where wise men
would be lost, and, in her days of weak-
ness, she found the fountain from which
flowed her greatest strength.

But Tom ! poor love is blind, and Tom
could not read the signs by which Sara
tried to show him many wondrous, new
things. He could not clamber over the
barriers, she herself had built, as his
trusting babies could. About his great
love for her he had drawn a cloak of
adament to shield the sacred treasure
from the sting of sharp, cruel words

which had pricked his heart, like thorns that could not be withdrawn, and which festered, bleeding still, behind the calm, cold surface.

He had not forgotten the face she turned upon him that fickle April day. It haunted his sleep and drove him to seek aid from those whom otherwise his manhood would have shunned, in the vain effort to give her back the glories of which he had robbed her. That it was he who gave them to her in the first place, seemed not to count. He had lost them— he had lost her—that was all! That she could ever change never dawned upon him. How could a woman change from hate to love? Only a woman can answer!

But the children understood.

And so, slowly, in stately graciousness, fair Summer drifted by, while Nature caressed dear Mother Earth until she yielded all she held, and the harvest was at hand.

CHAPTER III.

The world was five months older, and
nature had long since robed the earth in
summer garb. The hills were clad in
emerald freshness, and in their midst
nestled a picturesque house, which spread
its white wings like a bird sheltering its
young in tender protection.

A broad veranda encircled the house,
and in the distance a miniature lake
dimpled the earth.

In the windless twilight the echo of
children's laughter floated upon the air,
and at the sound a woman's figure rose
from the hammock cushions, and moved
slowly in the direction of the voices.

It was a pretty scene that greeted her.
The last lingering rays of the setting sun
were touching a hay stack into dull gold,
and a small brown farm house stood near

by, surrounded by little sheds, like an old hen with its brood of chickens, while solemn-eyed cows were chewing their cud, patiently waiting their turn to be milked.

The laughing voices proceeded from the big barn, and a shout of welcome hailed the approaching figure as she drew near.

" Look, look, mamma! We are lions and tigers, and we have caught papa and put him in our den, and now we are going to eat him all up!"

Two merry brown faces looked down from the pile of sweet-scented hay, and as she gazed up at them a tousled dark head appeared beside them. " I'm just amusing them a little, Sara," he said, deprecatingly, but the boys were down upon him in an instant.

"No! no! You can't go—we haven't eaten you up, yet!" they cried, and a rough-and-tumble game among the hay followed.

The weary expression faded from the

eyes looking on, and a faint smile grew in their depths as the shouts of delight made the rafters ring above her head.

" Catch him ! oh, do catch him, mamma !" cried Lawrence, as his father eluded him and sprang to the floor out of reach.

" No, sir! I've escaped now, fair and square, so the game is up," laughed the dishevelled victim. " Besides, it is tea time, and you boys must run in to be cleaned up a bit, or mamma won't let us play in the barn again," and he laughed once more as Danny turned a somersault in his efforts to gain the ground.

" I'll beat to the house," cried Larry, and away they scampered over the fields.

" Hadn't you better go, too?" asked his wife, glancing over his disordered dress. " You seem to have returned to your childhood since we came here ; you act like an overgrown school boy !"

Tom drew himself up and smoothed his hair. " The boys are so happy," he murmured, apologetically.

" Aren't you ever going to do anything
but play with them and lie round on the
grass?" she asked, and had he looked at
her he would have seen that she was
smiling. But he did not glance at her.
His eyes rested on the opal-tinted sky,
and he sighed wearily as he answered :

" I am making every effort to retrieve
myself, but things move slowly, and it is
good to forget—everything sometimes,
in a romp with the boys. They are such
dear fellows; it rests me to be with
them."

She looked up at him as he stood beside her. The witchery of twilight was
closing in upon them, and the still country air was sweet with the odor of a
thousand blossoms. The chatter of the
boys' voices reached them through the
gathering dusk, and the light from the
dining room streamed across the veranda with a cosy welcome. It was all
very peaceful, quiet, homelike ; and Tom,
as he stood with bared head, looked
oddly handsome in the mystic lights. He

turned towards her suddenly, as if drawn by the magnetism of her gaze, and their eyes met.

" This is all very tame and wearisome to you, Sara," he said, sadly. " But try to be patient a little longer and you shall have your baubles back again.''

He drew his hand across his brow and sighed heavily.

She moved restlessly and echoed his sigh.

" I wish I could make you happy !'' he cried, turning away, and entering the house abruptly.   '

" Tom !'' she called, but he did not hear, and the night wind caught a sob from her lips as she raised her face to the sky. " Why won't he understand? '' she whispered to herself.

" Mamma, do hurry, Janet has hot biscuits and honey for tea,'' and Lawrence drew her in to the pretty room, where the mellow rays of a hanging lamp fell upon the round table, with its white and gold china, and center piece of wild roses.

Danny was showing a newly found bird's nest, and eagerly describing its capture. " We can climb any tree in the orchard now, can't we, Larry?" he cried. " My! but we're glad you came here to live, papa; it's a heap nicer than that stuffy old New York. A fellow couldn't have any fun there."

" Yes, and besides, we never used to see mamma when we lived there," added Lawrence, " and now we have her all the time. That's the best part of it all, I think."

Tom glanced across the table at his wife, and her cheeks flushed under his gaze.

" Mamma was very busy in those days," he said quickly as he noted the hot flush.

" O yes, I know," answered the boy, "but I'm glad she isn't busy any more, because it's so nice to have her always with us, isn't it papa?" It was her eyes this time that sought the other's face, but he did not meet her gaze.

" We want mamma to be happy, my boy," was all he said, and with a sigh she dropped her eyes upon her plate and fell into a long revery.

The boys' voices grew dim in her ears, while memory carried her back to the first few years of married life when she had been the children's best playfellow, and the sunlight of their father's life. But when the money had come to them, she had lost her simple happiness in the glitter and glare of the world's delights, and missing the sweetness of life, had wondered, fretfully, why she was not as gay as the rest of society seemed to be.

" No, Danny boy, mamma is too tired to put you to bed to-night."

" But I want her to sing to me—she often does now."

The words roused her and she rose from the table. "Yes, I will take him," she said, lifting the sturdy little fellow in her arms, and turning towards the

door, with Danny's triumphant face
laughing defiance over her shoulder, and
Larry's arms about her waist. Tom followed them wistfully with his eyes, and
then turned out into the cool, dim night.

Nature lay sleeping under a silvery
coverlet of moonbeams. Peace walked
abroad, and the breezes whispered among
the tree tops with gentle murmurings,
lest they should waken the dreaming birds
that nestled among the leaves.

The shadows lifted from his eyes as
they dwelt upon the beauty of the scene.
" I will make her happy yet," he murmured to himself. "In such a fair world
pain and discontent can not live."

A soft, low voice stole out into the
night, singing a tender lullaby, and the
watcher outside stood listening until it
grew fainter and fainter, finally dying
away into the gentle crooning of a
mother-bird.

" God bless her !" he whispered under
his breath.

CHAPTER IV.

The clear notes of a bugle woke the echoes far and near.

"Good Heavens! That's a coaching horn, who can be coming?" A white-robed figure ran out into the glare of afternoon sunlight, shading her eyes with her hand, to gaze down the dusty high-way.

"Who is it?" called Tom, from the shade of the vine-clad porch.

"Ned Darnley's coach, and five, six, eight in the party. Oh, Tom! What shall we do?"

"We are no longer fashionable, so I don't suppose we can send word to them that we are 'not at home,'" he answered, with a flippancy his face denied.

"But I'll have to get something for them to eat!" she cried, in dismay.

"Well, they have come for country fare ; give it to them," he said.

"Honey and cream and eggs? Oh!" she faltered.

By this time the coaching-party had caught sight of the white figure on the steps and a cheer arose, mingling with the blare of the bugle as they swept up the drive and stopped before her.

"Here we are! You didn't invite us, so we thought we would give you a surprise party."

"Sara, my love, you have actually grown fleshy; I think I'll come for a summer boarder!" cried one tall, thin girl.

"Hello, Tom, old man! Lend a hand with these nags, will you?"

"Why, how pleasant it is here, Sara. I never thought it would be like this!"

"What did you expect to find?" asked Sara, helping to relieve her guests of their light wraps, and bringing out more cushions for the hammocks.

"Oh, a sort of farm house, you know,

surrounded by pigs and chickens and all
that ; but this is quite a charming summer
villa !"

Sara's cheeks grew warm at the tone of
condescension.

" It is very pleasant and we are not
disturbed by chattering neighbors," she
said.

" But don't you nearly die of ennui?"
asked another. " You were the gayest
of us all in town. I declare, it is too
bad to have you buried alive out here!"

" I don't feel buried!" cried Sara,
resentfully.

" We miss you awfully, my dear. It
is so deliciously gay this season," ran on
a third. " Of course, you have heard all
about the Adirondacks party; you were
to have been one of us, you know. Well,
it was simply perfect! Two swell Eng-
lishmen were in the crowd, one a younger
son of a Duke, awfully swell, you know."

" Grace thinks she has him," whispered
the first speaker in Sara's ear, " but he
is only flirting; he told me all about it."

"Helen Avery is making a dead set at Stanton Reeds. His wife died last spring, you remember, and Helen is already angling for his millions," said one of the girls, and there was a general laugh.

The men joined them later and they scattered into groups of two and three, while Sara vanished to consult Janet upon the condition of the larder. There was no use in attempting any elegance, so she decided to take Tom's advice and give them a simple lunch of country fare.

The boys brought her great bunches of roses and white wood violets, and she lingered about the table, arranging the flowers so as best to set off the quaint old silver and dainty china. She dreaded returning to the veranda. The gay chatter jarred upon her strangely and the world she had lost, once so all important, seemed oddly vapid, now that she stood outside the charmed circle. There was no end, no aim in it all. Only a dizzy whirling round and round in one narrow space. It reminded her of the senseless rotations of a whirligig.

She heard her boys go past, on their way to the berry patch, and, going to the window, she watched them as they trudged along, swinging a big tin pail between them. How brown they had grown, bless their merry faces!

"Sara, can I help you?"

It was Tom's voice and she turned to find him regarding her, wistfully.

"No, no," she answered, becoming conscious that there were tears in her eyes and hurriedly brushing them away as she smiled up at him.

"I'm going to take your advice and just give them berries and cream, with some of Janet's famous biscuits."

He laid his hand on her arm as she passed him. "I know this is all very hard for you," he said. "Your tears fall like lead on my heart."

"O, Tom! Can't you see——?" she began, impetuously; but a light laugh broke in upon them as one of the girls tripped in through the low window.

"Heavens! a scene of domestic bliss; how romantic!" she cried.

Tom left the room abruptly and Sara bent over the flower-strewn table.

" It almost looks like 'love in a cottage' to see you and Tom so spoony," she ran on carelessly. " I should think you would have to make love to your husband, if only to have a little excitement in this dreadful exile. You poor thing! We all feel awfully sorry for you, don't you know. I do hope Tom can come back to New York soon!"

Sara drew herself up proudly. "Your sympathy is wasted," she said. " I don't care to return to the life you think so fine. I have learned something better. I love this little home, and I'm not ashamed to confess that I love—my husband!"

The girl shrugged her shoulders and glanced about the simply furnished room. Sara caught the smile on her lips, and her cheeks flushed, but she said nothing, and the awkward silence was broken by Janet announcing that all was " aready."

It was not a very successful feast. The luscious honey went unappreciated, and the biscuits were only nibbled at, much to Janet's disgust.

Conversation languished and a feeling of constraint settled down upon them all. The guests were not at their ease. They had come, expecting to be received with gratitude, such as a ship-wrecked man would show the bright-winged birds that brought him tidings of the world beyond. But they had found a woman proudly content, who seemed to have fallen in love with her exile, and lost the sense of all of which she had been robbed.

They did not linger long after the simple repast was over, and, just as the young moon rose the coach drew up before the veranda.

" It's going to be a divine night ; let's drive home the longest way," cried one of the girls.

" Can't! Have a dinner on hand for eight," said another.

" So have I—do hurry, Ned," urged a third, as Darnley sprang to his seat.

" Well, good-bye! good-bye!" came the chorus of voices, and some one blew the bugle in a parting salute.

Tom and his wife stood within the shadows of the deserted porch, listening to the voices and roll of the wheels until they died away in the distance, and a sweet quiet fell upon the drowsy land. Then she drew a long breath, and raised her face to his.

"I can almost hear the stillness," she said, softly. " How good it seems after all that endless chatter and fuss!"

He looked at her tenderly.

" You have been a brave little woman to-day," he answered. " They came here to patronize and condole, and they went away thinking you were content, and had nothing to regret. I alone knew how the contrast of your present simple life hurt you——"

"O hush!" she cried. "Why are you so blind? Can't you see that I am not the same woman I was in those old days? Didn't you hear me tell Grace Osborne that I loved this little home, and that I loved——"

She broke off suddenly, and he drew closer to her side.

"You loved?" he asked, breathlessly.

"You!" she whispered, with a half-smothered sob.

"O, child!" he murmured, drawing her to him. "Have I won you back to me again?"

The shadows fell about them, and the moonbeams silvered the world as if the heavens smiled upon so rare a happiness.

"How is it that you have forgiven me?" he asked at last, gently lifting her face to his.

"I don't know," she whispered, smiling through her tears. "I think it was the touch of nature that healed my world-sick soul.

BARBARA'S EMANCIPATION.

NATURE was drawning over sleepy earth the soft gray curtains of twilight. The birds twittered drowsily to each other, and the butterflies kissed the roses in fond goodnight.

Suddenly the still repose of the garden was broken by a rush of feet, and a flutter of short skirts, as a tall boy dashed up to a giant old oak, and, throwing his arms about its trunk, cried, breathlessly :

" I told you so ! Pooh, you can't run !"

The short skirts now reached the same spot.

" I can run ! You know I beat you once, and I would this time if it wasn't for these nasty skirts that twist around my legs !"

Leonard laughed. " You're nice

enough for a girl, Bab," he said, adding, lest so much praise might be injudicious, "but you are only a girl."

Barbara threw herself on the grass. She was hot, tired and defeated. " I hate you!" was all she found to say, hiding her flushed face, and beginning to cry.

Leonard looked at her in disgust. "There ! that's just like a girl, as soon as you get beaten you begin to squeal. You're a regular cry-baby, you are !" and stuffing his hands into his trousers pockets, he trudged off, whistling, leaving Barbara to sob out her woe to the stars, as they twinkled at her from behind the cloud curtains.

Poor little Bab! Her one ambition was to subdue the play-fellow whose superior powers were at once her delight and her despair, and this last defeat, with the taunt he had delivered as a parting shot, filled her cup of bitterness.

That night she lay awake a long time, thinking out a plan which would rein-

state her in Leo's good opinion, and fill
him with admiration and envy, and before
the dew was off the flowers the next
morning, she was out in search of him,
eager to put her new idea into execution.

She found him seated astride a box in
the orchard, whittling and whistling.
He looked up as she approached, but she
checked any reference to her defeat of
the previous evening by saying :

"I'm going to ring the chapel bell!
Do you want to come and hear me?"

"Ho, ho!" laughed Leo. "You're
too much of a 'fraid cat to do that; it's
all bats and spiders up there."

Barbara shuddered inwardly, but did
not reply as she led the way to the
chapel, which had long been left to the
ravages of time, and now served as a
monastery for bats and owls.

Leo had often been tempted to ring the
old bell, but had never dared risk his
weight upon the worm-eaten ladders,
and his respect for Barbara grew momen-
tarily, as she persevered in the dangerous

feat. Rung after rung creaked under her feet, and her light figure swayed uncertainly with the bending ladder. Cobwebs brushed her face and clung to her hair, while big bats flapped their wings over her head, but a glance at the face below gave her fresh courage and at last she reached the bell.

Leo followed her with his eyes, hardly daring to breathe, but at last a dull dong-dong creaked out from the rusty old bell that had been dumb for years, and he threw his hat into the air, crying: "Hurrah! Bab, you're a brick; I didn't believe you'd do it!"

Triumphant and ·applauded Barbara looked down at him from her perch: " Who's a 'fraid cat now?" she cried, but as the words left her lips, the rotten timber gave way beneath her weight and she fell heavily to the ground at Leo's feet.

He shook her, calling her name in terror, but she gave no sign of life, and,

trembling with fear, he lifted her in his
arms and carried her home.

Mrs. Stanley saw them from the
window, and soon the house was all confusion.   Dr. Blick, however, brought
relief by assuring them that no more
serious damage was done than a sprained
ankle, and when Bab regained consciousness, it was to find herself a prisoner of
the couch.

Her rash venture had cost her dear,
and, of course, she cried ; Leo said girls
always did! Mamma's comforting only
made things worse, so Leo was sum-
moned, and came in looking shy and
sheepish. He had been commanded to
comfort her, so he said :

"I say, Bab, you're a regular trump,
you are, and you stumped me, you know ;
I was afraid to do it."

At these words, Barbara's tear-wet
face emerged into rainbow smiles.

"Really? You mean that, and you'll
never, never call me a cry-baby again?"
she asked.

"No, criss-cross my heart," answered Leo, and Bab was satisfied.

But as the summer days rolled by, while she lay on the couch or hobbled painfully about, she thought the price for her satisfaction a heavy one. Leo was very good—on rainy days, that is; but when the sun shown and the birds sang, Nature called him to come forth and be one with it, and he obeyed the call.

One day as Barbara lay on her couch, she heard her mother saying:

"My dear Clara, I can not bring myself to see the subject in anything but a ridiculous light. You know I think we women have already power enough, for, if men govern the world, we rule them by love? A woman's influence is limitless, it is God-given, and it ought to be all-sufficient for her needs."

Clara rose to leave. "It is just such women as yourself that are detaining our march to freedom. I have no patience with your blind content," she exclaimed.

Mrs. Stanley was smiling when she

returned to the room after bidding her friend good-bye, and Barbara claimed her attention at once, demanding an explanation of the subject of woman's emancipation. She was delighted with it and saw glorious visions of the future, when she should rise to Leonard's level.

"How long will it take to come true?" she asked.

But her mother only laughed, and said she hoped it would never come true.

"Well, I'll get emancipated as soon as I can and wear trousers, and have short hair and ride my pony straddle, and beat Leo at everything," Barbara declared.

"Wait and see," was all her mother answered, but she smiled to herself as she spoke.

So the days rolled on until Bab could walk about as well as ever, and then a dark cloud rose over her skies, for Leo was to be sent across the seas to Oxford, and she would not see him for many long years.

The decision was sudden and the departure came quickly on its heels, so, before Barbara realized all it meant, the good-bye morning arrived, and she and Leo were together for the last time.

She clung to him, while he stood straight and awkward in her embrace; and, of course, she cried, though Leo wished she wouldn't, because it made his own throat feel so lumpy. Finally, he made an effort to put an end to the shower.

"O, I say, Bab! Never mind. Just you get emancipated while I am gone, and then knock me out every round when I come back."

This brightened her, even in the present crisis.

"That's what I'll do, Leo; just you wait and see," she cried.

Leo seized this opportuniny to beat a retreat, and turning round in the carriage waved his hat at the forlorn little girl who followed him with tearful eyes until he was borne out of sight.

But the picture she made dwelt with
him through the years that followed, and
the memory of that loving farewell kept
guard at the door of his heart.

CHAPTER II.

" O, mamma, just think ! dear old Leo is coming back at last ; why, he must be here now !"

" What are you talking about, Barbara ?" said Mrs. Stanley, glancing across the breakfast-table to the flushed face opposite.

" About Leo ; this letter has been delayed and he says he will be here by the fifteenth ; that was yesterday, so he may drop down on us at any moment !"

" I hope you won't quarrel as you used to do."

" Oh no, I'm too old to be teased now," said Barbara.

" I don't know about that," answered her mother, smiling quizzically.

" But I am going to be very dignified, and show him that I am a grown woman

and not a silly girl any more. He told me
to get 'emancipated' when he left, and
I'm going to show him that I am !"

"Ah, Barbara, that's the same spirit
which made you climb the belfry six
years ago. Don't let it bring you to grief
as it did then."

" How could it ?" she asked, pushing
back her chair.

" Come, Don, we must go for a run,
you lazy dog ; the birds are calling to us."

Outside, in the sweet-scented garden,
the sunbeams welcomed her as one of
themselves ; kissing her cheeks into
blushes and touching her hair with warm
caresses.

" O ! it's so good to be alive, Don,"
she whispered, lifting her head to greet
the breezes. " This is where we used to
play together, Leo and I. You were
only a puppy then, Don, so you can't
remember, but I do ! This old cherry tree
was our favorite place, and we would sit
on that stone wall while we ate the cherries we had picked. There are some up

there now, and I'm going to get them for
the sake of old times."

She gathered her skirts about her and
began the ascent, reaching the top of the
wall at last, breathless, torn and dishev-
eled. " O ! how much easier it used to
be," she cried. " Don, you keep watch
below; I wouldn't be caught like this
for anything."

The cherries were as good as of old,
however, and Barbara was enjoying them
to her heart's content when the dog
startled her by springing to his feet with
a low growl.

" Don !" she cried, nervously.

"Don't be frightened, it is only I,"
answered a reassuring voice, as a young
man emerged from the shadows. " Your
mother told me I should find you here."

Barbara's head swam. " Leo?" she
asked, faintly.

"Of course ; I hope you don't need an
introduction ? I should have known you
anywhere, but it seems especially natural
to find you—up there !"

The girl's cheeks burned. She gathered her fallen hair in one hand and drew her feet under her torn gown. It was too provoking to be caught like this, when she had planned to meet him in all the new dignity of her womanhood. She caught the old teasing twinkle in Leo's eyes, and it was more than she could bear.

" It's hateful of you to steal on me like this," she burst forth. "You are just the same horrid boy you used to be !"

" Leo leaned against the tree. " You didn't use to think me horrid, though. I remember when you bade me good-bye—"

" O ! how rude of you to remind me of that !"

" I wouldn't mention rudeness if I were you," he continued. " You have abused me ever since I appeared and after an absence of six years, and considering I have come so many miles to see you—"

"To see me!" she interrupted, scornfully.

"And, as I said before, considering the fond hopes which your affectionate farewell gave—"

An exclamation of anger interrupted him.

"Well?" he asked.

"Go away!" she said.

"Why, I have just come, and if you could see yourself, you would understand the reason I enjoy staying! The picturesque disorder of your hair is—"

"Will you go?"

"I'm sorry to disoblige you, but I really can't tear myself away," he said, laughing up into her angry face.

"Then I shall!"

"Take care," he cried, but her impetuous movement loosened the stones beneath her, and she was precipitated into his arms, an ignominious bundle of torn clothes, roughened hair and fallen pride.

She struggled to free herself, but he

would not loose his clasp. "Don't be angry, little Bab," he whispered.

"Let me go!" she cried.

"Not till you have given me a welcome home," he answered.

"Well—what shall I say?" she asked.

"Don't say anything; just look up at me."

"I will, if you let me go."

"Don't bargain, look at me!"

"I won't till you let me go!"

"And I won't do that till you look at me!"

"Then we'll have to stay here forever!" she cried.

He laughed again. "I don't mind," he said.

The moments dragged by. Don snapped at a fly, and startled Barbara with the fear that some one was coming to catch them in this absurd position. She made one more effort to free herself, but in vain.

"Leo, you ought to be ashamed of

.

yourself. Let me go!" she cried, the
angry tears filling her eyes.

"I am only waiting for you, Bab,
why are you so afraid to look at me?"

"I'm not afraid!" she asserted.

"Then prove it."

"Will you let me go if I do !"

"Surely !"

"Well then—there!" Her eyes met
his at last, and a moment later she fled
from him with burning cheeks. "How
did he dare?" she whispered to herself.
"Oh! the wretch!" She tried to slip up
to her room unseen, but her mother
caught her as she was running upstairs.

"Did you see Leo, my dear? I sent
him to find you an hour ago."

"Yes, I saw him."

"Then why didn't you bring him back
with you. Why child, what makes your
face so red?"

"It's—it's so warm," murmured Bab,
confusedly, and vanished upstairs to hide
herself from questioning eyes.

An hour later she emerged from her

room, with cooled cheeks and a determination to revenge herself upon the presuming old playfellow. She felt she had made a bad beginning in the renewal of the friendship, and she was angry with herself and him. As the days rolled on, however, she found it almost impossible to avoid him for her mother always welcomed him with cordial affection, and encouraged his frequent visits.

CHAPTER III.

"I have asked Leo to dine with us to-night, Barbara," Mrs. Stanley said, one afternoon at luncheon. "He has grown to be such a charming fellow, that I feel as if we did not see half enough of him."

Barbara fidgeted. "But why did you have to ask him to take dinner with us?" she asked.

"My dear child, it is the least I can do—you seem to forget he has been away six years. What is the trouble? Are you sorry he has returned?"

"N—no; that is—I think I liked his letters better!"

"I don't wonder you miss those charming weekly budgets." Mrs. Stanley observed. "They have been almost as good as being with Leo himself all these years, and have helped you to keep pace with the change in his character that time has brought about."

"I think his character has deteriorated," said Barbara, lifting her chin in the air, but her mother laughed.

"Nonsense!" she answered.

When Barbara came down stairs that evening she wore a black satin dinner gown that added ten years to her age, and her hair was piled high upon her head. During dinner she was unusually silent, and amused Leo by the dignity she assumed.

"Do you still believe in the emancipation of women?" he asked, as they rose from the table. "I remember your ideas of old, especially the attractive costume you proposed to adopt."

Barbara flushed with annoyance. "Those were the wild absurdities of a child," she said. "Of course I don't advocate masculine attire, but I most certainly do believe that men must yield us our rightful place at their side, and, though you laugh now, I am positive our day is coming, and we will do wonders then!"

Leo laughed. "I don't doubt that; women are great wonder-workers," he said.

"She will accomplish her work not as a woman, but as an intellect——"

"Heaven forbid," he murmured, and Mrs. Stanley exclaimed: "Do stop talking nonsense, Barbara, my dear, and give us some music."

The girl shrugged her shoulders, but seated herself obediently. "What shall it be?" she asked.

"'Love's old Sweet Song,'" suggested Leo, smiling into the face so near him, but she would not meet his eyes, and began a difficult fugue which left no room for sentiment. This new Barbara amused him for one evening, but as the days went by without bringing a change, he began to lose patience. Had it not been for the scene in the garden he would have feared that the Barbara of old was lost in the present unapproachable young woman, but the memory of her eyes that morning gave him hope, and day after day he strove to break down the wall she had built about herself.

At last the dread that she really disliked him grew in his heart, but, though suspense was well nigh unbearable, he sought in vain for an opportunity to put his fate to the test.

One afternoon, when Nature seemed hushed to sleep by the drowsy lullabies of myriad-winged creatures, Leo lounged aimlessly under the leafy shade, recalling old memories which the scene brought back to him.

Here it was that Bab and he used to picnic with goodies stolen from the pantry shelves, and over yonder was the old chapel where she had nearly lost her life in the effort to win his approval. Poor little maid! He had been rough and unkind to her in those old days, but now——"ah, Bab! You are more than avenged upon me," he said, aloud.

"How am I avenged?" demanded a

voice behind him, and he turned to find himself face to face with the object of his soliloquy.

" Shall I tell you ?" he cried.

" No, no !" she said, retreating. " I don't want to know. After all, I—I feel sure it would not interest me !"

" But you shall listen. You have tormented me long enough. Barbara, I——"

Barbara turned and fled.

" She sha'n't escape me this time," he exclaimed, and started after her in hot pursuit.

Away they went, over the flower-kissed meadows in as mad a race as of old, and, as in those days of childhood, Leo out ran Bab.

" There !" he panted, as he caught and held her firmly. " I have won another race, and you—you yourself are the goal. O, Bab! why did you run away from me ?"

She was too breathless to reply.

" Is it because you dislike me—have I

changed—or—Barbara! do you love some
one else?"

Her hands fluttered in his like frightened birds.

" I don't love any one," she faltered.

" You must love me," he cried. " Don't
you know that the thought of you has
been my guiding star all these years?
Don't you know the memory of my little
Barbara has kept me true, so that I could
come back and not be afraid to have her
read my heart?   Oh, Bab! don't say you
can't love me—I couldn't bear it!"

She drew her hands from his. " I don't
hate you, but——"

"Don't say ' but,' " he exclaimed.

" What shall I say?" she asked.

" Say ' I love you!' " he pleaded.

She walked a short distance from him
and then paused.

" Are you sure you think I am as good,
as clever as any man ?" she asked.

" Don't trifle, Barbara."

" Answer me," she insisted.

" Yes, yes, of course.   You are as far

above every man as an angel could be," he
replied, coming nearer.

" Do you think me a hoidenish school-
girl?"

" Absurd !" he exclaimed, impatiently.
"Do you?"

" No, no! you are the most charming
woman on earth," and he drew close to
her side.

" Will you promise never, never to
tease me again, or—or——"

" Barbara! you are crying !" he cried,
and caught her in his arms.

"Well," she murmured, after a pause,
" it's nothing new for you to make me
cry.   You always did."

"But I never will again," he said.
" The old days of tyranny are over, and
you are my queen now, little Bab, so
I will obey you as a faithful subject
should."

Barbara crept closer to his side.

" Ah! but my great plans for the
emancipation of women?" she sighed.

Leo laughed softly.

" What more can you what than to conquer the conquerer?" he asked. "Isn't that victory enough ?"

" Ah! but it was love that did it," she sighed again.

" Are you not glad?" he whispered.

And the sunbeams laughed as they heard her murmur "Yes!"

A TWENTIETH CENTURY ROMANCE.

S HE stood surrounded by a group of black-coated men, like some pink-lipped marquerite, blossoming midst meadow weeds.

"You need not look as if you were sorry," she was saying. "You know you will all forget me a month after I have gone!"

"That's like a woman's ingratitude," cried one. "Here we've been dancing attendance upon Miss Elizabeth Dare since she first 'budded.' I dare say every man-jack of us has proposed at least once, and now she accuses us of fickleness and insincerity!"

The girl shrugged her shoulders. "It's no such great honor to have you propose; that is just a little habit you have of encouraging each 'bud' as she appears.

What would you do, though, if some 'innocent' should really accept you ?"

" No use arguing, Dan ; a woman will have the last word—even the 'new woman' refuses to let go that inheritance from mother Eve !"

"They are no good, anyway," Dan asserted, angrily.

Miss Dare laughed. "Don't be rude. I'll give you this two step if you want it and will promise not to be cross to me."

" Thanks, no !" he answered, bowing mockingly. "Dick Osprey's name is on your card for this, and I see him plowing his way toward you over toes and trailing gowns. I don't care to meet Dick in a duel, even for your sake !"

She turned to meet Osprey, and as she took his offered arm, a tall, slender man of about thirty, with soft, brown hair and quizzical eyes brushed past them, nodding to her carelessly in nonchalant greeting.

The light suddenly went out from her face, and her gaze followed the debonair form until it was lost in the crowded rooms.

"What a detestable jam!" she said in a tired voice. "It's impossible to dance here!"

"Let's go into the library, then—awfully jolly place there; they've fixed it all up for spoons," suggested her companion.

"But we are not 'spoons,'" was the irritated reply. He glanced down at her whimsically. "No, but that is your fault," he ventured.

"Naturally, you would flirt with any one; quality is not important!"

He whistled softly, but did not speak till they were cosily hidden behind one of the nooks of palms in the library.

"Everything is all wrong with you to-night, Beth, what's the trouble, anyway?"

His question let loose the pent-up feelings and she broke forth, impetuously:

"Oh! To-morrow I leave this place. It's been 'home' to me always, yet, I know that no one is really very deeply

sorry to have me go. No one will miss
me. No one will fall asleep longing to
see me, or wake in the morning saddened because I am no longer here! It
will be the same in New York, too. I
will make many 'friends' (so-called) and
be very gay, but there will be no one to
care! I am not to blame, people are
not to blame; it is because we all lead
such unreal lives that this is so! Society
does not love, nor feel, nor think! There
are so many of us in her ranks that, when
one sinks, or drops out, the human tide
sweeps over them instantly. and their
places are filled. They are forgotten!
No one has time to remember! We are
so gay, so busy with pleasure. There are
so many to laugh with you, but none to
weep! Oh, I'm sick of it all! I wish
Daddy and I were going to some quiet
place where we could lead real lives
among people who lived and loved, suf-
fered and enjoyed. I am sick of all this
glitter, as a child that has nauseated itself
on candies!" She paused abruptly, as

if remembering she but wasted words, and sighed restlessly.

Her companion looked uncomfortable; this was so unlike her, and he felt confused.

" Ah, well! It's not quite as bad as all that, you know," he began, soothingly. " You are all upset to-night, you see, and things look queered. But just think of the chaps that can't get into our crowd and who would think it was cheese and pie to have cards to this ball, don't you know?" He laughed. "That's the way to feel contented with your lot—to look at the poor devils who can't get where you are, don't you know?"

She broke into a short laugh. " True, I had forgotten! What's the joke?" drawled a lazy voice near by, and she raised her head eagerly.

" Dick has been giving me a lesson in social ethics," she answered, looking up into the face above her with an expression, which anything—short of a man— could have read at a glance.

" Yes, Beth got on the war-path.
Rather scared me, by jove! You ought
to have seen her, Mont. But I brought
her to reason, all right," he added.

" Good for you, Dickie! The man
who can bring a woman to reason has——

"Not been born!" broke in the girl's
voice, mockingly.

Dick rose. " She's too much for me,
to-night; see what you can do with her,
Mont!" and he moved away with a
laugh.

Montgomery Blair settled himself
comfortably in the vacated seat. "This
is nice!" he sighed, resting his head
against the pillows at his back, and gazing at her with his peculiarly winning
smile. " I'm glad to get the chance of a
little farewell chat with you. When do
you go? To-morrow?"

She turned away from him, and was
pulling to pieces the green leaves at her
side. She nodded assent to his question
without speaking, and he idly watched
her work of destruction as he talked on.

"It's hard on us fellows to have you
go, you know. You are far and away the
jolliest girl in the crowd. It will seem
beastly queer not to find you on the
links this spring,—you and I make such
a team at golf, you know. I don't suppose you will take a run out to Water-
bridge this summer? That's bad—thought
perhaps I'd see you there, any way. Remember how I ran down there every
Sunday last year? Good fun, wasn't it;
remember that night we got lost from
the others, and—oh, why—I say—what's
up, Beth?"

She had buried her face in her hands
and was crying bitterly, but silently.
Never before had he seen her in this
mood. He watched her in dismay, helpless, awkward, sorry, puzzled, and wondering what he had said to make her
cry. Always, during the several seasons,
he had known her only as a gay society
girl—one of the many he knew and liked,
as he met them upon the frothy crest of
the social tide. This unprecedented ex-

perience left him speechless and amazed, and at a loss how to proceed. At last, unable to bear the sobs which shook her slender form like a wind-tossed flower, he ventured to lay his hand lightly upon her head, and, to his satisfaction, this proved a beneficent remedy, for the sobs gradually grew less, until they ceased altogether, and the girl lifted her bowed head with a nervous laugh.

"Here, take my handkerchief—it's bigger," he said, solicitously, pushing his cambric into her fingers.

"Do you feel better?" he queried anxiously, as she handed it back to him.

She laughed again. "Oh, yes, I'm all right now. Don't look so appalled. I won't do it again. You thought I could only laugh, didn't you? I'm sorry I was such a goose as to show you I could do anything else. Please forget it. I—I'm just tired, that is all."

"You don't often do that, do you?" he ventured.

"Oh!" she cried suddenly. "You don't

know me at all! For years we have
waltzed and golfed together, yet you are
as ignorant of the real me as if we had
never met!"

He looked sobered, "That is true,
Beth, I have never known you. I wish
now that I had."

She laughed bitterly. "Don't deceive
yourself," she answered. "You would
never learn to know me if we spent a
hundred seasons together. You could
never know me any better than you have
in the past. It's impossible in the air we
breathe."

"I would try," he began.

"No, you wouldn't," she interrupted.
"You would soon get bored. No one
can be serious in cap and bells—it is out
of place. One must laugh if one will go
to the minstrels. Even love—look how
we treat it—we marry for every reason
under the sun but for that!"

He smiled. "Love! It is hard to think
of you as falling a victim to the little base
god," he said.

She paled and rose to her feet. " Of course not. I can neither love nor suffer. I am only a butterfly."

" I didn't mean——" he stammered.

" Good-night," she interrupted, "and good-bye."

He took her hands in his as she stood beside him. "Good-night, Beth. I'm a clumsy idiot. I seem to hurt you every time I speak to-night, but, well, I won't forget you, dear, and I wish I had another chance at knowing you! Good night, don't have the blues. You are really an awfully lucky girl, you know. Good night, and good luck to you."

" Good-bye," she whispered, bending her head to hide her face. " Good-bye."

CHAPTER II.

In two years there is time for many changes. Time for the rise and fall of nations—time for birth and death—for grief and joy—for all that goes to make up life and history.

But the two years that had passed since Elizabeth Dare departed to make her home in New York, had left Montgomery Blair as untouched as if Time had forgotten him, and on this December morning he sat at his desk with only a pucker of annoyance to crease his smooth brow.

The swish of silk skirts pausing at his door, made him glance up.

" Heavens ! What a scowl, dear boy. What's wrong?"

He pointed to three open letters before him. " My morning mail," he said.

"One is filled with an account of the illness of a chap I know; gone abroad for his health. Another informs me of the death of an old college chum of mine, and the third treats of the loss of a fortune! Nice lot of news, isn't it? Death, disease and disaster. Quite cheering."

His sister laughed. "It's the way of the world, my love!"

He looked at the bright face and richly-clad figure before him. "Not of your world!" he muttered.

"Is Jack in his office?" she ran on. "I want to see him. We had an argument at breakfast. Jack says I scatter too much of his filthy lucre. It's odd, isn't it? But Jack always sees only my faults! I have to recount all my virtues for his benefit, every now and then, just to keep him from forgetting I possess them. It's so very bad for a man (a husband) to be one-sided in his views of such things, you know—it's apt to make him narrow and close. But he's had time to digest the long list of my virtues, with which I furnished him this morning, so I'll run in to reap the reward before he recovers from the effect.

" I see—a check—he's doomed ; poor Jack !"

" By the way, who's the friend who lost the fortune?" she asked, pausing on the threshold.

" It's a girl—Beth Dare—remember her?"

" I should say so, and how she fell head over heels in love with——"

She checked herself suddenly, with a laugh.

" Beth in love? With whom, for heaven's sake?" cried her brother in amazement.

" Oh, never mind, stupid, she wasn't in love with anybody. I was joking. But I thought her father went to New York to make his everlasting fortune. How has she come to grief?"

He shook his head. "She doesn't explain ; she only says she finds herself 'with nothing to exist on,' and begs me to find her something to do. Hard luck, isn't it? Deuced awkward, though. What am I to write her? I don't know of any place where a girl like that could possibly be placed, do you, Reta?"

She looked suddenly thoughtful. "I'll think about it," she answered, moving away, and he heard her enter Jack's private room, further down the corridor.

He picked up the girl's letter and re-read it. It ran :

"Probably you have forgotten me, but, you see, I have not lost sight of you, and now in my desperation, I turn to you for help. I find myself left with nothing to exist upon, and I want you to get me some sort of work that I can do. I love children, as you know, especially boys and I think a position such as a governess, or companion, to invalid or delicate children, might be possible for me. In fact, this is the only thing I am at all fitted for. Perhaps your sister, Mrs. Costelli, might know of some such

place. Do ask her about it and let me
hear from you soon.

Yours, as of old,

" ELIZABETH DARE."

"She takes it most uncommonly cool,"
he muttered, "most girls would be in
tears over such luck, but Beth never was
the 'weepy' kind!"

Then, as if contradicting this thought,
his memory leaped back two years to the
night they had parted in the library, and
he lost himself in a maze of puzzled con-
jecture. A woman's nature is like a
Chinese puzzle to the ordinary masculine
intelligence.

The closing of a distant door roused
him from his revery. "Well?" he queried, glancing questioningly at his sister,
as she paused in the open doorway.
"Had Jack digested the virtues satisfac-
torily?"

She nodded, waving a check before
his eyes.

"It's bigger than I expected. Jack's

a dear, and he says you can write Miss Dare to come to us at once, to look after Glendening, you know. Jack's a softy where Glen is concerned, and he jumped at the chance of getting such a companion for the poor boy."

" By jove! just the thing! What a dummy I was not to think of that! She said she thought, perhaps, you could suggest some such place for her!"

An odd expression flitted over Mrs. Costelli's face, and she laughed quizzically. "Oh well, we live in the days of 'thought transference', " she said, gathering her skirt preparatory to departure. " You can write her to come, anyway, she'll be a God-send to our poor little invalid. Tell her to come when she chooses, the sooner the better!"

But her brother paused twice as he wrote the letter, to wonder why she went away with that queer smile puckering her mouth.

CHAPTER III.

A week later found Montgomery Blair, buttoned to the chin in his big fur-lined overcoat, pacing up and down the station, waiting for the express from New York. He smiled to himself in the dark of the winter's night at the position in which he found himself, regarding his old friend. Unconsciously, since the arrival of that letter of appeal, he had felt strangely responsible for the weal or woe of the girl, and the feeling gave birth to an odd sort of tenderness which surprised and made him half ashamed. The plucky spirit with which she faced misfortune roused his admiration, and the lonely, forlorn condition of the brave little woman touched the hidden springs of chivalry in his nature, and made him vow within himself that he would do his utmost to make her life more bearable.

The shriek of the approaching train put an end to his musings, and he tossed away his cigar as the engine thundered into the station.

As he stood, peering anxiously in the wrong direction, a laughing voice at his elbow made him glance down to find the object of his search regarding him with joyously dancing eyes. He clasped her hand warmly, wondering at her courage in facing this new life.

"You are looking awfully well," he began, as they leaned back in his sister's coupe, and the glad ring in her answering laugh almost startled him. He had expected, at least, the gloom of a resigned spirit. All during the drive home he regarded her with a puzzled stare, which brought a flush to her cheeks and added to her charm. Once, or twice, he tried to broach the subject of her changed fortunes by a delicately sympathetic touch. But she avoided the topic, evading his

questions by simply replying that there
was enough to provide for her father, in
his old age ; and, for herself, she hoped
to be able to be happy in the new existence before her, but she did not care to
talk about a matter which must be more
or less painful.

Her dauntless courage won his hearty
admiration—a woman with pluck always
appeals strongly to a man—and he was
heartily sorry when they drew up before
his sister's door. The drive had been a
unique experience, and one that was dis-
tinctly pleasant.

They found Glendening sitting bol-
stered up among his pillows, watching,
with childish impatience, for the arrival
of the person who was to belong exclus-
ively to his own self. They had been good
friends in the past, when Beth occasionally stole up into his room to tell him
stories on the rare occasions when she
visited at the house, and the boy had not
forgotten her during her two years' absence. Now she was to be all his own,

and, when she bent above him to whisper, "We will begin to live and be happy, now, Glen—just you and I together," he threw his arms about her neck, and drew her face down to his with a sob of gladness.

"I'm all right now, Daddy," he said, later on, when his father carried him off to bed. "She's the stuff, you know. I shan't mind not being like the other fellows, as long as I can have her!"

CHAPTER IV.

Beth fitted into her new life as if crea-
ted for it. She and her little crippled
charge were left unmolested in their cosy
quarters, for Mrs. Costelli was immersed
in the surging tide of the season, and
found little time to visit Glen's sanctum.
When she did run in on them for a
breathless moment, however, she mar-
velled at the look of sweet content in the
girl's face, wondering how she could so
easily resign the glories of her old position in the world.

As for Glen, his thin little face lost its
expression of pathetic patience, and
caught something of the eagerness of
youth and boyhood.

They always had something absorb-
ingly interesting on hand. Now it was
photography in which Beth grew profi-

cient, and took snap shots of every object within range of the little 'hawkeye', while the developing of the pictures was an endless delight to Glen.

Then it was the collecting of foreign stamps, a field which furnished inexhaustible joys to the invalid, and had the added attraction of being an interest he could share in common with "the other fellows."

Montgomery, true to his resolve not to let "the little girl" feel her changed position any more than could be helped, managed to drop in on them very often, until it became a settled habit for him to spend a half hour, or so, with them nearly every afternoon.

There grew to be something peculiarly attractive to him about that square, sunny room, which Beth had filled with plants, in whose growth and blossoming Glen had become as interested as she herself. Two canaries sang joyously in their gilded prisons—a lesson for Glen, to which she often pointed out the moral, especially

on those days when his affliction seemed
unbearable.

And then there was Beth herself, sweet
as the flowers and contentedly joyous as
the birds, and bright as the sunbeams
themselves! Always ready to help, to
sympathize, to condole or to rejoice;
as restful, as wholesome as Nature herself.

But Montgomery did not analyze—he
enjoyed!

" Why do you come to see me so much,
now, Uncle Mont?" questioned Glen,
one snowy afternoon, when Mr. Blair
had "dropped in" earlier than usual.

Beth was popping corn over the red
coals glowing in the grate, and the flickering light danced in her eyes and flushed
her cheeks, while a sudden dimple tucked
itself into the corner of her mouth at the
boy's abrupt question.

" You're an impolite young gentleman !" declared his uncle. "Aren't you
glad to see me, I'd like to know?"

Glen nodded. "But you never used

to come at all!" he persisted. " Why do you do it now? Is it 'cause Beth is here, Uncle Mont?"

Beth here interrupted the catechism with a little cry; the popper had rested too near the amorous coals and the fluffy, white kernels were blazing themselves into charred, black balls. Montgomery rushed to the rescue and by the time the fire had been extinguished, Glen had forgotten his questions in new interests, while he munched contentedly, on the rescued remains of the popcorn.

" Well, this is cosy!" cried Jack Costelli, breaking in upon them, in snow-powdered garments.

Beth sprang up. " Oh, do come in," she cried, brightly, whirling a big armchair into the circle about the fire. " Glen was just wondering why you had not been in to see him to-day."

Jack nodded to Mont, and bent tenderly over his boy.

" Did you miss the old Dad, even with Miss Dare showering you with attentions? You rascal! There, there is a reward for your noble behavior!"

He tossed a package of foreign stamps upon the couch, and sank into the armchair with a sigh of contentment.

" Snow outside, but warmth and smiles of welcome inside; that's what 'home' should feel like, eh, Mont?"

Blair nodded; he had been thinking something like that himself, lately.

" I wish there need be none out in the snow," murmured Beth, wistfully, raising her eyes to the window, where the shadows already gathered; then she busied herself with the tea things, putting in a word now and then, as the others talked.

" There's mamma!" cried Glen, as the bang of a carriage door reached them through the snow-muffled air outside, and the rustling of silk skirts told them the mistress of the house had returned. A moment later and she entered, breezy, bright, beautiful. " Heavens! how cold

it is," she cried, stretching her hands over
the fire and glancing about the group.
" How 'homey' you all look; quite
pastoral! You are doing Glen worlds of
good, Miss Dare. You never miss me
now, do you, love?"

Glen's face flushed slightly, but he made
no answer, and she turned away again.

" Well, I can't be lazy, I must rush off
and dress for the dinner at the Bluche's;
have you forgotten, Jack?"

Costelli yawned. " Ye gods, no!" he
answered, irritably. " One can't forget
when you are about, Reta !"

" Hurry !" she called back, as she went
down the hall.

He rose reluctantly. Beth, at the tea
table, was pouring out the steaming,
amber-hued liquid into the egg-shell cups,
with their bits of sugared lemon in the
bottom.

" Not time for even one cup?" she
asked.

He shook his head, looking longingly
from the threshold at the group about

the fire. Glen, nestled like a contented
bird in his feathery nest, counting his
new stamp treasures, and Montgomery,
stretched lazily in the lounging chair,
sipping Russian tea, while Beth fluttered
about, ministering to them both, as the
masculine nature loves to be ministered
unto—unobtrusively, but absolutely !

" I'm deuced glad I don't have to climb
into my tuxedo," Jack heard Montgomery drawl; "I don't recollect ever
being quite as comfortable as I am at
present," and Beth's glad laugh broke
out, as if he had said the wittiest thing
imaginable.

One evening, not long after, as Blair
was in the midst of dressing, to go
through with the different engagements
of the evening, he was suddenly overcome by a sense of distaste, of weariness,
for the social treadmill, and he paused in
his preparations to gaze at his half-clad
reflection in the glass, with a look of
disgust.

" What an ass you are !" he muttered.

" You're playing the part of a court-fool; skipping and bowing, and scraping and grinning to people who don't care a rap for you, and who only smile upon you because you happen to have stemmed the tide—so far !''

His thoughts reverted to the big, cosy room, which was beginning to influence him strangely. He saw Beth's golden brown head as it bent over Glen, brightening the boy's pale face with the sunshine of unselfish love. Only two years ago and Beth had been one of his comrades in the paths of pleasure ; now she was poor and forgotten. So it would be with him if he dropped out. What was the use of it all, then?"

A sudden longing for something real, and true, and lasting surged over him. He flung aside the dress suit and slipped into his business coat. " I'll go up there and surprise them," he murmured, smiling to himself.

It was after nine when he reached his sister's house, but a light still burned in

Glen's sitting-room. Montgomery crept stealthily to the half-open door and looked in. A big fire crackled and sputtered on the andirons, and Glen lay on his couch, his eager face turned towards Beth, as she sat on a stool beside him.

" But it wasn't so!" she was saying, her voice low, and sweet, and full of feeling. " The big giant Despair was really and truly killed, after all, and who do you suppose it was that killed him?"

" The monster fiend?" questioned the boy, breathlessly.

Beth shook her head. " Oh, no! It was the beautiful and gentle lad we called Love, you know."

Glen opened wide his eyes. " But he was a little chap, and almost as useless as I."

The listener outside was fascinated by the expression on the girl's face as she answered softly, " Yes, he was a little lad, but all things are possible to Love, my darling."

The boy sighed, and then smiled. " I

see," he whispered. " Your story means that I can do just as much good in the world as if I were like the other boys. I'll try to, Beth, like the little lad called Love, just for your sake!"

She nestled her face against his. " Just remember, sweetheart, that to Love all things are possible," she whispered.

Montgomery's eyes felt moist, somehow, and he would have been glad to slip away unobserved, but as Beth rose she saw him, and he had to come forward.

" I cut the gimcracks to-night," he explained, lucidly. " They bore me, any way. I'm all out of gear, and came to you two to get smoothed out. Isn't it late for the old gentleman to be sitting up?"

" Very, but we got so interested we forgot about going to bed."

" I'll carry the chap up to-night," Montgomery said, lifting the frail little form in his arms.

" Oh, wait," cried the boy, as he felt

himself carried away. "I want to say good-night to Beth."

The girl blushed slightly, and shook her head. Glen said nothing, but the wistful eyes filled with slow tears, and unable to stand that, Beth came close, the flush deepening in her cheeks. Glen's head rested against his uncle's broad shoulder, and she was obliged to stand on tiptoe to reach the little invalid's trembling lips. Her veiled eyes were not lifted, but, as her hair brushed against the tweed coat sleeve, a wave of hot color flamed her face, forehead and ears, while Montgomery was astonished to feel an odd sensation stir in the depths of his being somewhere.

CHAPTER V.

"Hello! old chappie, where the mischief have you been lately? Missed you at all the doings this past month. Every one wondering what's come over you. Why are you fighting shy, anyway?"

"Been busy," Blair replied, shortly.

The other whistled, then laughed. "When a fellow like you gives that excuse there is the deuce and all to pay," he said, adding, sotto voce, "generally a woman in the background, you know."

"Hold your tongue!" Blair growled, frowning. "Because you are up to that sort of thing is no reason every other man must go the pace."

"Whew!" his friend regarded him thoughtfully. "It must be a genuine love affair, then. I wouldn't have guessed it of you, old chap. Congratulations, cards out, all that?"

Blair wrenched himself free from the detaining grasp, and strode along with crimsoned face and furrowed brow.

" By jove !" he muttered, " the ass hit it right, after all. I'm in love with her and I didn't know it myself !" he laughed. "I didn't know what it was ailed me !"

He suddenly became conscious that a bird was singing happily near by. He raised his head and saw the gay crocuses springing through the sodden earth. Spring had come !

" I'll go and tell her," he whispered to the spirit of spring which caressed his forehead. " I'm not good enough for her, I know that, but I want her to know about it, anyway."

It seemed as if his feet were winged, and he had never reached his sister's home so soon.

Beth was singing, so were the canaries, and Glen's couch had been drawn into the square window, where he could catch every sunbeam..

" Oh, hello !" he cried, gleefully,

catching sight of his uncle. "How jolly
you've come ! Now he can tell us that
story he promised us last time, can't he,
Beth?"

Her smiling glance met his across the
couch.

"This is an early call," she said.
"Glen and I were just wondering what
we could do that was fitting for this
glorious spring morning, and you come."

"Am I a fitting guest for a ' wonderful spring morning?'" he questioned,
eagerly.

She lowered her eyelids in sudden confusion, and his heart-beats quickened.

"But tell us the story—the story!"
Glen's voice grew impetuous, and Montgomery, looking across him at the down-
bent head, took a sudden resolve.

"All right, young man, I'll tell you a
story about a man who was a—fool!" he
began.

"What was his name," queried Glen.

"His name ? oh, well, we will call
him Despair."

"O! is it about the Giant Despair that Beth knows, and the little lad called Love?"

"Yes, but this man was not a giant—there was nothing great about him; he was only a fool, and he led a fool's life."

"What sort of a life is a fool's life?" broke in the boy.

"You will never know it—be thankful that you will be spared that, at least, my boy."

The sober tone silenced the child, who glanced inquiringly into his uncle's face, but the eyes above him were bent anxiously on the top of Beth's head, as it rested, half hidden in Glen's pillows.

"So this fool lived on for many years," Montgomery continued, "and what he thought was content and happiness, grew more and more burdensome. On his back was strapped a bundle like a peddler's pack, and in this he carried Pleasures. It was a heavy bundle, for it held all the fool possessed in life. He fancied it was very valuable, and never felt the weight, or weariness of carrying it about, until a strange new feeling stole over him, and then the pack of Pleasures began to drag him down, and he longed to rid himself of the burden which he no longer treasured. But it was not easily to be disposed of. The witches' 'Habit' and 'Custom' had strapped it tightly to him, and the magic spell could only be broken by the touch of a little lad called Love. But when Love drew near and looked into the fool's eyes, Love shrank away, and would not touch him, because the poor fool had wasted his life, and was not worthy of Love's cares and comfort."

" Oh, but I don't believe the little lad called Love would ever be so mean !" cried Glen, impetuously. " Beth says he is beautiful, and forgiving, and sweet, and she says, you know, 'that all things are possible to Love!' "

Montgomery leaned over the boy's couch and touched the bowed head on the pillow. " Beth, is it so ?" he whispered, tremulously.

She sprang to her feet, and for one instant he saw her quivering, tear-wet face. · " Oh, no ! no ! It cannot be. You don't understand. You won't care to have it so when you know everything. Oh, why did I come—oh, why—it was wrong—it was wicked——"

The incoherent words were lost in a burst of tears, and she turned and fled.

Montgomery's face was white. He tried to smile as he met Glen's startled gaze, then he broke down and, burying his head beside the boy's, he cried, brokenly. " It's all up with me. I knew it. I knew I would never get her. I'm not good enough."

Glen's little life had been spent in the companionship of pain. Perhaps, that was why he comprehended this anguish that was beyond his childish understanding. His sympathetic silence and the tender touch of his thin little fingers, as they strayed over the bowed head, brought a strangely sweet comfort to the bruised and aching heart of the man, and when the weak voice, whispered softly, " Never mind, uncle Mont. Don't feel so sorry. I'm not good enough for her, either, but she loves me, you see," a sudden hope sprang into life and blossomed.

The bowed head was raised. " You blessed little comforter," whispered the husky voice. " You give me a new thought to take hope on. I had forgotten it was the way of angels to raise, and to love, fallen man !"

CHAPTER VI.

But hope is as elusive as brilliant, and Montgomery lost the vision in the long night, when all the world slept, and he alone kept vigil with himself. Happy is the man who can look the past steadfastly in the face, in the solemn silence of the night, and not shrink back in shame, regret, remorse.

The morning found the watcher in a fit of depression which promised all sorts of horrors for the yellow journalism, but the timely arrival of a thick, daintily-scented envelope saved him. He tore open the seal with trembling fingers and plunged into the letter with devouring eyes.

" My dearest," he read. The words danced before him, he re-read them, then a wild glance at his hat told how his heart flew to the writer of those two magic words, but another glance at the closely written sheet chained him to the spot.

"Yes, I will call you so. This once only, though, for when you have read this confession you will not wish to have me love you !

" When you have read it to the end, and are angry and disgusted with me, oh ! just try to remember this—that I loved you—and do not judge me as I deserve ! I have deceived you. I am an imposter, there it is, out at last ; now despise me !

"My father never lost his money, but oh, Mont ! I grew so sick of it all. I was so tired of the sham and falsity, the insincerity and unreality of such an exist- ence, that I could not endure it any longer ! Then, to be honest, at last, I was homesick and lonely for—for—oh, how hard it is to tell—for you ! There now, despise me some more ! I never thought it would be so hard to tell you !

"It seems so much worse now than it did when I planned it all out in New York. I suppose the life I have led here with dear little Glen has cleared the moral atmosphere about me, and I can see more clearly than when I was still in New York. But there is nothing to excuse me, just nothing! I deceived you. I schemed to get back here! Oh, Mont! I cared for you all the time in those old days; even that first season I came out. But it was only nonsense between us, always; nothing but the silly chatter that one forgot the next day. Everything was a jest. It never occurred to you that I was a woman, with a woman's heart. You were gay with the rest of our little world and I had to be gay, too! Yet all the time my heart was so hungry for love; for your love, and I used to think if only we could be in earnest for one short day, you might love me! It was all this which troubled me that last night; do you remember, Mont? And ever since I have longed so to be back!

But not as in those old, fretted days. Just as I have been in these past beautiful months, when you and I and Glen have lived real lives, and learned to read our own hearts and to know each other. So I planned it all; but I never actually lied to you. I never said father had lost his fortune. You remember I only said I had nothing to exist on, and that was true. I was starving for the real things of life!

But I had not lived this sweet, beautiful life then, so I did not realize the monstrosity of my actions. Now I do, and I know you can never, never forgive, or love such a creature as I! This will be a long good-bye. I have tried to prepare Glen for my leaving him, as of course I shall, as soon as possible. You will be glad never to see me again.

Father thinks I have been visiting here. I shall simply slip back into the old, detested routine, while all these happy months will sink into my heart like dreams too beautiful to be real. I expect to be gone before to-morrow night.

Good-bye! Good-bye! This confession has wrung my heart, my pride, my self-respect, but it was your due and had to be made. Now you know me as I am, and all I can ask you for is your forgetfulness!

Good-bye!   "BETH."

The letter fluttered to the floor. Montgomery raised his head and caught the reflection of his dazed face in the opposite mirror. Then the meaning of it all rushed over him, and he caught up his hat with the shout of a boy.

Once more his feet seemed winged as he sped towards his sister's and let himself in with his pass-key.

Beth's voice he heard, reading aloud to Glen, as he ran up the stairs two steps at a time. At the sound of the opening door, she sprang to her feet, and the book clattered to the floor. Had she expected him? Who knows?

He laughed as he met her frightened eyes, and, reaching her side, he took her into his arms, regardless of Glen's interested stare. He laughed again, as he lifted her chin in his hand and forced her to meet his gaze. "You little criminal!" he cried. "You small cheat! You unblushing man-hunter!"

Then Beth saw a sudden mist fill his eyes, and, with an answering sob, she buried her face on his shoulder, while he whispered, brokenly, "Oh, God bless you, true heart, you have torn away the tawdry curtains which hid the true happiness, and shown to me the real meaning of life,—and of love!"